Fly Fishing
the
Tailwaters

Ed Engle

• Stackpole Books •

Published by
STACKPOLE BOOKS
Cameron and Kelker Streets
P.O. Box 1831
Harrisburg, PA 17105

Printed in the United States of America
10 9 8 7 6 5 4 3 2 1

First Edition

Cover design by Caroline Miller
Interior design and typesetting by Art Unlimited

Library of Congress Cataloging-in-Publication Data

Engle, Ed, 1950-
   Fly fishing the tailwaters/by Ed Engle. -- 1st ed.
      p. cm   ISBN 0-8117-2343-7
   1. Trout fishing. 2. Fly fishing. I. Title. II. Title:Tailwaters.
   SH687.E67 1991
   799. 1'755--dc20   90-10233
                                                         CIP

This book is dedicated to the South Platte River

Contents

Introduction

FLY FISHERMEN LEARN EARLY on how elusive truth can be. It appears that any laws—at least in the precise sense that there are laws of gravity and thermodynamics—do not govern the lives of trout. At best, most anglers end up with a lifetime list of some of the times and ways trout like doing one thing better than another.

If I ever thought I had a lock on fly fishing the tailwaters for trout, compiling this book has cured me of it. I've learned through conversations with anglers across the country that fly fishing the tailwaters is as detailed a business as it gets. I've also heard a few tales about those days that happen once or twice in an angler's life. Days where conditions are perfect to the point that the trout seem to come to the angler rather than the other way around—the kind of day where you knock off early because your shoulder is sore from playing fish (I'm a sucker for sore shoulder stories). Either way, days astream are what dreams are made of. The one point that everyone seems to agree on is that fly fishing the tailwaters can be one of the most productive fishing experiences you ever have—whether for trout or dreams.

What you will find in these pages is one fly fisherman's tailwater discoveries. Some of the entries should apply to your own home tailwater fishery, some of them probably won't, but if any of them gives you new ideas on how to go about things or helps to add an entry or two to your lifetime list concerning the quirks of trout, I'll be happy.

There have been a number of people who have kept me honest while I was working on this book: John Gierach, Dennis Breer, Kent Brekke, Don Schmier, A. K. Best, Neill Peterson, Chas Clifton, Mike Lawson, Roy Palm, Ric Munson, Dr. J. V. Ward, Dr. Jay Windell, and Clee Sealing.

Special thanks to my wife, Monica, for sticking with a fly fisherman who talks in his sleep about mayfly hatches.

Ed Engle
Palmer Lake, Colorado

CHAPTER 1

The Paradox

I T DOESN'T TAKE LONG to understand there's a paradox to all of this. Here you are on a wonderful, shimmering river casting a fly over the biggest trout you've ever seen in your life when you realize that the reason it's possible is because there is a dam upstream from you. It doesn't make sense at first. The river exists, as you know it, because upstream there is flat water? A reservoir is making all *this* possible? Nonsense!

As a rule I don't lie awake at night trying to solve fly fishing paradoxes, but take a river like the San Juan below the Navajo Reservoir in the northwestern corner of New Mexico and it can get you to thinking. It's rough, dry country out there. Sagebrush, piñon pine, and juniper dot the land. The cottonwoods down along the river where Simon Canyon comes in look more like the "hanging" trees in an old western movie than the benign providers of shade for weary anglers. All in all, I'd say the San Juan looks more like a hideout for desperados than the home of law-abiding trout.

But the trout are there, let there be no mistake. And they weren't always there, either. Figure that before the days of introduced trout and the regular runs of stocking trucks, the occasional Rio Grande cutthroat might have made its way as far south as Simon Canyon or may even have come *upriver* that far from the Colorado River near the Grand Canyon. It's more likely, though, that the natives preferred the river farther north, up in the headwaters and its tributaries in the San Juan Mountains near present-day Pagosa Springs, Colorado.

The trout that are below the Navajo Dam today are introduced species, most commonly rainbows, although browns and Snake River cutthroats have also been stocked on occasion. They are there simply because water released from the reservoir into the river has created a suitable environment for them. "Suitable" might actually be a little on the conservative side. A 6-inch fingerling rainbow trout will normally grow about a half-inch a month. Biologists expect these trout to measure around 12 inches long their second year in the river. A three-year-old will be about 17 inches and a four-year-old will average 21 inches and 3 1/2 pounds.

For a river that historically didn't have much going for it in the way of trout, those are some pretty husky fish. They are there for absolutely no other reason than Navajo Dam and the water backed up into the reservoir behind it. And there you have it—the paradox.

Rivers that occur below dams are commonly referred to as *tailwaters* or *tailraces*. Tailwater trout fisheries, which occur in many of the states from east to west throughout the United States, may represent some of the best trout fishing in the nation. The controlled release of water from a reservoir into the river below often moderates extreme runoff conditions, provides for increased water flow during dry periods, clears the water, and provides higher levels of nutrients that allow the river to produce more and larger trout than it would if it were free running. In many cases, like the San Juan, where water is being taken from the lower, colder layers of the reservoir, fisheries biologists are in the position of creating a trout fishery where virtually none had existed before simply by introducing trout into the new cold-water habitat.

When it comes to fly fishing for trout, I cut my eyeteeth on tailwaters. As luck would have it, I lived about forty-five minutes away from the South Platte River in Cheeseman Canyon. At the time I didn't really care that the Platte was a tailwater. In fact, I'm not even sure that I realized it *was* a tailwater. All I knew was that you could see the trout nudging around in the bottoms of the pools and in the glassier glides, and that I wanted them. I wanted them for all the reasons that any fisherman wants a fish.

The trout in the South Platte were difficult taskmasters. Difficult to the point that I started hanging around Bodmer's Fly Shop in Colorado Springs looking for the answers that might lead to my first South Platte trout. If you subscribe to the "stage" theory in a fly fisher's life you would call this the "days spent in the wilderness" stage. I was the kind of case that when I left the shop, old George Bodmer would quietly say

A tailwater or tailrace is the river located below a dam. The release of water from the reservoir has a profound effect on the tailwater fishery below it.

to one of his sidekicks, "He's got it bad, doesn't he?" and maybe shake his head a little.

I think I got my first trout on the South Platte early in my second season as a fly fisherman. I still remember that it nailed a #12 or #14 soft-hackle on the swing where a chute came into a big pool. If I'd "had it bad" before that trout, I ended up with "it" a lot worse afterwards.

With time I began to learn some of the South Platte's secrets. I picked up on a funny looking burnt-orange fly called a Des's Shrimp that worked miracles on the river during the high water in the spring. I paid my dues on the midge hatches for a couple of years before I got the hang of catching trout on tiny flies. After a while I got the feel of a method of fishing nymphs that everyone was talking about. They called it the South Platte method, or dead drift nymphing. All in all, I began to feel like I was getting my feet on the ground.

Of course, by this point things had gone from the simplicities of sport into the realm of hard-core tailwater fanaticism—the sort of thing where I got off from work at five on Friday afternoon and by ten minutes after five I was in a souped-up van speeding toward the Miracle Mile on the North Platte River in Wyoming or taking off over the mountains en

Diversion dams are used to direct water into irrigation ditches in the western states.

route to the Frying Pan River. The drill on these trips invariably required that we stuff our faces full of burgers and fries as often as possible on the way to the river because we all knew there would be time only for fishing and sleeping when we got there. I'm glad I did all of this when I was young, because I know it would kill me now.

Along with learning where to get the best burgers between Colorado Springs and just about every major trout river within a thousand miles, I learned a little about rivers. I learned that free-flowing, undammed rivers or those that we fished far downstream from a dam fished differently than those miles of a river that were directly below a dam. More importantly, I came to realize that some of the tricks I'd learned fishing the South Platte in Cheeseman Canyon worked *very* well on many other tailwaters I came across.

I began to notice some similarities in the species, sizes of the species, and hatch times of insects among the various tailwaters. In many tailwaters there seemed to be more aquatic vegetation than in comparable free-flowing rivers. The tailwaters didn't show the signs of spring "blow-outs" that were so common on many of the free-flowing western rivers I'd fished. It also seemed as if there were more and larger trout in the tailwaters. These trout were often easily spotted in the water because of a characteristic clarity that occurs in certain types of tailwaters year-round except during periods of high water in the spring. Obviously, none of the tailwaters fished *exactly* the same, but there were often enough similarities to make what you learned on one of them somewhat applicable on another.

I also found that when it comes to figuring out tailwaters the best place to begin is at the dam itself.

Dams come in all sizes and shapes and are built from a variety of materials depending on the purpose the engineers had in mind when they designed it. Although there seems to be an infinite variety in the appearance of dams, at least to the casual observer, when fly fishing for trout in the tailrace below any particular dam the two most important aspects are the location of the gates used to release water from the reservoir and the schedule on which the water is released.

The gate location and the depth of the reservoir determine the temperature of the water released into the river below. Water-release schedules depend on whether a reservoir is being used to divert water for irrigation, store water, or generate electricity.

DIVERSION DAMS

The least complex type of dam is quite common on trout streams in Colorado where I live. These are the diversion dams that the irrigation ditch companies use to divert water from streams or rivers into their ditches. On the smaller streams, like the St. Vrain Creek, which runs through

Lyons, Colorado, the diversion dams are as simple as a concrete wall built across the stream channel. These small dams create enough of a head to form a small beaver-pond-size pool where the water is diverted into the gated irrigation ditch. The dam itself has no real gates since its only purpose is to build a head of water. Any excess water simply drops over the top of the dam and into the river below. For that reason it's called a surface-release dam.

On a stream the size of the St. Vrain it's difficult to tell if the diversion dams have much effect. I certainly wouldn't consider the stretches of river below them tailraces in the truest trout fishing sense of the word; but think about the effect they're having on the river. They act very much the same as a series of beaver ponds or natural lakes. These small impoundments could possibly be affecting water temperatures both above and below the diversion dams. There is no question that water temperatures are affected in the bigger water diversion projects in the West, like the Colorado River for example.

Water temperatures are affected because of a characteristic found in most temperate-zone lakes and reservoirs. These bodies of water, if deep enough, have seasonal cycles of water temperature changes. In the summer months the water stratifies (technically known as summer stagnation) into layers according to temperature. The top layer of water, or *epilimnion*, is warmest and therefore lighter in weight and stays on top. A middle layer called the *thermocline* has a lower temperature than the epilimnion and consequently doesn't circulate with it. The third layer, or *hypolimnion*, is the coldest and is located in the deepest parts of the reservoir.

In the autumn the reservoir "turns over" when temperatures in the epilimnion cool to the temperature of the hypolimnion, which dissipates the thermocline, and the surface winds mix the entire lake. As the water continues to cool because of lower air temperatures a funny thing happens. It expands, becoming less dense and consequently lighter, when colder than 4 degrees centigrade. The colder, less dense water remains on the surface where it often forms ice. The reservoir then stratifies into layers where the somewhat warmer but denser water at 4 degrees centigrade is near the bottom of the reservoir during the winter. In springtime the ice melts as the surface water warms to 4 degrees centigrade and once again causes a turnover when the now denser water sinks to the bottom. Finally, the cycle begins anew when warm layers of water begin to form over colder, deeper layers in the summer.

What this means in relation to diversion dams is that, at least in the summer, the warmer layer of water is flowing over the top of the dam, which means the water in the river below will have somewhat elevated temperatures. The water in the reservoir above the diversion dam may be a bit cooler since it's storing less heat.

Now that I've put you through the science of it, I'll admit that I've noticed very few differences when fishing for trout around diversion dams and just fishing my favorite undiverted streams. If I had to make comparisons, the only thing I would say is that it appears to me, and this is shaky at best, that the streams around diversion dams often are what we call "caddis" rivers in the West, meaning that caddisflies are a dominant trout food but by no means the only one found on the river.

Actually, what I've most often noticed about the smaller diversion dams is that some pretty good trout seem to end up in the deep, steadily flowing waters of the irrigation ditches. I've been known to make a few casts to them, too. One of the saddest sights I ever saw happened in the fall one year on the day they closed the gates to the irrigation ditches. The ditch rider, in a pair of waders, walked the ditch with a pitchfork and bucket. He eventually filled the bucket with beached brown trout that weren't able to escape back into the river. There were some good ones, too.

One final remark about diversion dams. On every river where you find them there will be stories about the hog trout that live up in the scoured-out recesses under them. It's obvious *why* they choose these places—it is absolutely impossible to get a fly, lure, or even a worm into them. Just try it sometime. The run of the currents and the backwash mix everything up and if you are lucky enough to get an offering to where it counts the odds are that you won't be able to detect a strike even if you get one.

These monster trout are almost always brown trout and in every community that has a diversion dam you'll hear stories about the big trout that lives under the dam. I never much believed in them—faith is a requirement when it comes to the uncatchable hog-trout mythology of the West—until the day they electroshocked the St. Vrain River. This is the kind of stream where a 10-inch or 12-inch brown is not a bad catch at all. It turns out that there was an 8-pound brown under the diversion dam!

BOTTOM-RELEASE DAMS

If a certain image comes to a fly fisher's mind when the word *tailwater* is mentioned, it's probably of the river below a deep-release dam. These are dams where the gates are located at the bottom of the structure and draw from the coldest and deepest layers of water except when the reservoir is experiencing the relatively short periods of seasonal turnover. These are also the dams that make tailwater fisheries for trout possible on rivers like the Colorado below Glen Canyon Reservoir at Lee's Ferry in Arizona or the Dolores in Colorado.

These western rivers are all located on the fringes of the range where trout could survive. Any natural populations were probably comprised of native strains that tended to be rather small in size and not particularly numerous in these borderline areas of their range. These marginal areas for trout were also the places where tremendous seasonal variations occurred in river flows that ranged from a summer trickle to springtime blowouts caused by spring runoff from the Rocky Mountains.

Historically, eastern tailwaters, like the Delaware River or the Chattahoochee just outside of Atlanta, that occur below bottom-release dams didn't hold trout for reasons similar to those of their southwestern counterparts. Trout, which tend to inhabit colder and better oxygenated upland waters, simply couldn't survive in the warmer, broader, and slower-moving low altitude rivers of the East. The construction of water-storage reservoirs along these rivers with dams that released cold water from the reservoirs' bottom levels created suitable habitat for trout.

What these examples demonstrate, both East and West, is a basic axiom about trout rivers in temperate-climate latitudes. You will find that as you move farther south in latitude the really big, broad trout rivers invariably will be tailwaters that are supplied with cold water from the bottom of a reservoir.

There is quite a bit of variation among bottom-release or deep-release dams and their tailwaters across the country. The typical profile, at least from the trout fisher's viewpoint, most often occurs in the western states where dams were built across deep canyons to gather snowmelt from the mountains. The water in the tailrace below these usually deep reservoirs is typically very cold in the first few miles. These are the kind of systems most trout fishermen think of when they think of a tailwater. Places like the South Platte River, the Bighorn, the North Platte's Miracle Mile, and the San Juan.

As you move across the country toward the eastern seaboard, considerable variation appears in the nature of the reservoirs behind the dams. This can affect the characteristics of the tailwaters below them. Tailwaters in the more mountainous regions that gather snowmelt may be quite similar to Rocky Mountain tailwaters. Other tailwaters occur below the dams of broader rivers that are gathered into relatively shallow reservoirs. These tailwaters exhibit a somewhat different character because the water in a broader, slower river tends to be warmer. Another twist are tailwaters like the West Branch of the Delaware, where in the late spring, high water temperatures sometimes stress trout populations. Cooler water from the reservoir is actually released into the tailrace to bring water temperatures *down*. A range of other variations appears among these examples.

This means that the well-known "typical" tailwater profile that many anglers recognize in the Rocky Mountains may not be present in some tailwaters in the East and for that matter along the West Coast where the reservoirs may have different thermal characteristics. As a rule of thumb, the colder the water coming into the tailrace, the easier it is to predict the trout fishing characteristics of that particular tailwater. As the temperatures go up the predictability goes down.

WATER FLOW RATE EFFECTS

The effect of colder water released from the bottom of a water-storage type reservoir is considerably more complex than just supplying life-giving colder water to a population of trout. Of considerable importance is the fact that the rate of water flow from the dam tends to be more constant than it would be in an undammed river. In springtime during peak runoff, water is being stored in the reservoir while in the hotter, drier months when the river's flow rate would be expected to be lower, stored water is released to meet demand downstream.

The more uniform flow rates below the dam affect the river in a number of ways. Stream banks, which tend to get hammered by spring spates, stabilize and provide a foothold for streamside vegetation that in turn provides sites for the adult flying forms of aquatic insects to rest and use for cover. The vegetation also supplies nutrients in the form of organic matter when leaves fall into the river and provides habitat for terrestrial insects. The more uniform flows encourage aquatic insect and other desirable trout food production because the bugs are using less energy maintaining their positions in changing current conditions. The same applies to the trout themselves, which spend less time fighting spates and more time feeding on the large populations of bugs. Ultimately, all this translates nicely into bigger trout.

If you've spent much time wading in the tailwaters the odds are that you've bought yourself some felts for the bottom of your boots. It always seems like the wading is just a little more slippery in the tailwaters, particularly those below the water-storage reservoirs. There's a reason for it, too. Not only does the more uniform flow created by the water releases encourage the growth of algae and other aquatic vegetation, the water itself, which is clearer due to the regular flow, promotes added growth of plants because the clearer water makes more light available for photosynthesis. The additional aquatic vegetation provides habitat for a several types of life forms that can greatly increase the growth rates of tailwater trout.

The water that is drawn from the bottom layers of a reservoir tends to be rich with nutrients from all manner of organic debris that finds its way to the reservoir bottom. These nutrients supply a ready food source to aquatic insects, scuds, aquatic worms, and snails that are in turn a major food source for trout. In some cases available food for trout in these tailwaters is truly incredible and results in phenomenal growth rates.

I clearly remember the first time the richness of a tailwater hit me. I'd been occupying myself with the trout in the South Platte River downstream from a town called Nighthawk. I knew the fishing was

18   *Fly Fishing the Tailwaters*

good there and that the river at Nighthawk was somehow affected by the dam farther upstream in Cheeseman Canyon, but I really hadn't made any connections.

The more I fished the South Platte the more I began to hear about the fishing up in Cheeseman Canyon itself. It was the sort of place that put new words into anglers' vocabularies; words like *cosmic, nirvana* and, I hesitate to say, *orgasmic*. In other words, the fishing was very hot in the three or so miles directly below the dam before the river swung into the private waters of the Wigwam Club. It had to do with the actual chemistry of the tailwater and with the special catch-and-release regulations that the Colorado Division of Wildlife had imposed on the water.

Getting into Cheeseman Canyon entailed a walk of a mile or so on the Gill Trail, which came in high above the river on the west side. I still remember the first time I swung around a bend in the trail and the river came into view below. The long, gliding pool, which I later learned was known as the Icebox Pool, was directly below me. Even from high up on the trail I could see the trout stacked up in there like cordwood.

I remember making the kind of calculations a fisherman is prey to. I thought to myself that I must be at least a couple of hundred feet above the river and easily a couple of hundred yards away from it and some of the trout *still* looked huge. I figured the brutes down there would have to go 20 or 24 inches. That meant the "babies" were probably 14 or 15 inches! It put a little lift in my step. I have never gotten over that vision of trout.

WINTER WARM AND SUMMER COOL

A final point needs to made about bottom-release dams and the rivers below them. The seasonal constancy of uniform flow rates creates what biologists call winter warm and summer cool conditions. This means that reservoir stratification causes summer water temperatures to be lower than they would be in an unregulated stream, whereas winter water temperatures will be warmer. In many cases the season's highest water temperatures on this type of tailwater may be delayed until well into the fall when the reservoir turns over. It also means that over the course of a year water temperatures in tailwaters don't vary as much as those in unregulated rivers.

These differences don't appear to have major negative effects on anglers or trout. In fact, in the states where it's legal, anglers can fish for trout in a river setting almost year-round. Most tailwater fisheries seldom freeze in the first two or three miles below a bottom-release dam. Water temperatures tend to be a bit warmer because the warmer water is on the bottom levels of a reservoir when it stratifies in the wintertime. What is affected are the populations of aquatic insects below the dam. For some species it means a population boom, but for others that require a wider range of water temperature cues to develop it can mean a decrease in numbers or even total elimination from the tailwater ecosystem.

HYDROELECTRIC DAMS

Probably the most difficult tailwater systems to figure out are those that occur below dams utilized to generate hydroelectric power. The most important factor in whether or not a specific hydroelectric tailwater will amount to much as a trout fishery has to do with the severity of the changes in flow rates. If water flow rates are being altered severely during power generation and the water is then released into a channel shaped like a rifle barrel, you can figure that the fishing may not be too great.

Other systems, where flow rate fluctuations aren't too extreme and the water is released into less severely configured channels, can provide surprisingly good fishing once you get used to the idea of fishing in a river where water levels can change abruptly. You get used to little intrusions into the serenity of things as simple as the Blue-Winged Olive hatch—like the sounding of the siren on the Philpott Dam on the Smith River in southwestern Virginia. The siren means get out of the river right now because a wall of water is on its way downstream and we don't care if you've been babying an 18-inch brown trout on a 6X tippet for the past fifteen minutes or not.

As a general rule look for power generation along with maximum water discharge to occur during weekdays with a reduction in flow on weekends and at night. Anglers who do their homework and call ahead to check power-generating schedules have little to fear.

An interesting aspect of the hydroelectric tailwaters is that while they appear to be the opposite of the more benign water-storage reservoir systems in that there is less bank stability and more turbidity, they still provide a measure of protection from spring spates that can be more severe than hydroelectric tailwater flows. Also, like bottom-release water-storage systems, they can provide the water temperatures and nutrients necessary for trout to grow where they would not naturally occur. This is particularly true in a number of hydroelectric tailwaters found in Kentucky, Arkansas, Missouri, and Tennessee. Not only do these rivers support trout (rainbows and/or browns in most cases), but in some cases they support trophy trout. The White River in Arkansas is a case in point and is known nationally for very large brown trout.

The Green River below the Flaming Gorge Dam in Utah is an example of a number of elements characteristic of tailwater trout fisheries. The dam, which is sometimes used to generate hydroelectric power during peak periods, has been known to cause fluctuations of as much as five hundred cubic feet per second (cfs) in as little as ninety seconds, which keeps wading anglers on their toes, so to speak. Despite the irregularly timed and sometimes extreme fluctuations in flow (dangerously extreme if you happen to be wading at the wrong time), the Green is known as one of the most productive trout rivers in the United States. A survey in 1986 estimated as many as twenty-one thousand trout in the first mile below the dam.

DAMS THAT MIX WATER

There is an offshoot of the bottom-release dam that is multi-gated and can "mix" water from various levels in the reservoir to produce optimum water temperatures on an almost year-round basis. You will find that many of the newer dams have been outfitted with mixing towers, whereas the older dams will tend to be of the bottom release variety. What the mixing towers do is bring back some of the diversity of insect life that is lost in bottom-release systems. The higher average water temperatures can also promote faster growth rates in the trout.

The Flaming Gorge Dam, which was built in 1962, started off as a bot-

Special regulations, such as catch-and-release fishing, are used by fisheries managers to maintain the quality of heavily fished tailwaters.

tom-release dam. At that time water temperatures tended to remain in the 40s for the better of part of the year. Although trout production and growth rates weren't shabby, they weren't what they are today, either. In 1978 a mixing device was added to the dam which allowed warmer surface water to be mixed with the colder deep water. Water temperatures after the addition of the mixer ranged between the mid-40s and mid-50s. The higher water temperatures increased the diversity of the insect life in the river, which in turn dramatically increased the growth rates of the trout.

CONTRADICTIONS IN PARADISE

What it all comes down to—whether you're talking about surface-release diversion dams, water-storage reservoirs with bottom-release gates, or hydroelectric dams—is that under the right circumstances any of these various types of tailwaters can become a rich trout fishery.

The fact is that there are any number of tailwaters across the country that are considered "blue ribbon" by anglers and fishery biologists alike.

Fly Fishing the Tailwaters

Many of these fisheries are considered so important that special regulations such as catch-and-release, slot limits, use of artificial flies and lures only, fly fishing only, use of barbless hooks only, and reduced bag limits have been imposed to protect and enhance the fishery. There is even research that indicates it is actually the combination of special regulations and the unique physical characteristics of tailwaters that work together to create a quality tailwater fishery. Special regulations are a good idea for another reason, too. The word can get around pretty fast about where the fishing is superlative. Even as productive as some of these tailwaters are they can't withstand the unregulated pressure of fifty thousand or one hundred thousand angler days per year.

Ultimately, it all really does come back to the paradox. The fishing *is* good down below the dam because of the reservoir. It's the cold water and the nutrients; it's the cooler summer water temperatures and warmer winter water temperatures. All of it works together to grow more and often larger trout depending on how a tailwater is regulated. A lot of fishermen draw a parallel between tailwaters and nonthermal spring creeks. I see the connection but I can also see that the two aren't *exactly* the same, either. Maybe the tailwaters are as close as we'll ever get to a completely man-made spring creek.

The paradox of fly fishing tailwaters really struck me when the Two Forks project on the South Platte River was being debated. I won't go into details. There have been volumes published on the pros and cons of the dam that the Denver Water Board planned to build on the South Platte River, but as of this writing the Environmental Protection Agency has vetoed the proposal (of course the veto is on appeal). The bottom line for me was that this particular dam would have put the portion of the river where I caught my first trout on a fly under eight hundred feet of water. It also would have flooded out Cheeseman Canyon and the wonderful fishing there.

On first analysis it all seemed straightforward to me. I am a river fisherman and this dam was going to wreck the river. The problem was that further thought complicated things. Actually, the Two Forks Dam would have flooded a *portion* of the South Platte, in fact, that portion that flows out of the bottom of Cheeseman Reservoir. How could I be against one dam but in favor of another that has contributed to the wonderful tailwater fishery that I cut my eyeteeth on? Actually, there are four separate tailwaters on the South Platte that offer productive trout habitat. Two of those tailwaters, the one below Cheeseman Reservoir and the one below Spinney Mountain Reservoir, are world class. The remaining two below Antero and Elevenmile reservoirs aren't exactly shabby, either.

I can't answer why one dam is good and why another isn't. I think there's a point to be made for having *some* free-flowing water between reservoirs that the Two Forks project would have eliminated. A superlative tailwater fishery will be lost if the Two Forks project goes through. I'll have to admit, though, that in the darkest moments of the Two Forks controversy the thought crossed my mind, once or twice, that maybe trout that live by the reservoir (or more precisely, below the reservoir) die by the reservoir. Anyway, I'm okay now.

What swayed me on Two Forks was simple loyalty. I've fished Cheeseman Canyon for close to twenty years. I've caught a trout on one day that still had the fly stuck in his jaw where I'd broken him off a few days before. Over the years I've seen generations of trout come and go in the canyon. It's something you just don't give up on.

Oh, by the way—the flip side of the coin—I can remember when the biologists released the first fingerling trout into the Dolores River below the newly completed, multi-gated McPhee Dam in southwestern Colorado. Few trout had survived that far down on the river until that very day. Now there exists a fine trout fishery. I often wonder if some fisheries technician with the Colorado Division of Wildlife threw his hands up toward the heavens after he'd opened the gates of that first stocking truck when they brought it to the river and shouted, "Let there be trout!" I hope so.

Stream surveys indicate that many tailwaters are highly productive trout fisheries.

CHAPTER 2

Professor Ward and the Bugs

W HEN IT COMES TO CULTS, fly fishing isn't much different than most. Simply put, this means that enough is never enough. With luck you can reach a pleasant level of mellow fanaticism and maybe even hold down a regular job at the plant. But there is a trout bum that lurks in every one of us and I think we all secretly know that a sparse little lean-to under the bridge, say on the Henry's Fork of the Snake River, is never more than a cast away. That would, of course, probably require that the family get together and send a deprogrammer with a spinning rod to bring you home.

A gang of us just like that spent our time trying to unravel the secrets of the South Platte River. We'd fished it for some time before we began to realize that it was a tailwater. As we increasingly concentrated our efforts in the Cheeseman Canyon area, which was right below Cheeseman Dam, it became obvious that the dam had an effect on the fishing. That was plain to see just by the sheer number of trout.

It took a little more time and some diligent keeping of fishing logs to figure out why all the trout were in the canyon. It began with the midges for me. I'd had some experience fishing unregulated freestone rivers and had never noticed so many midges. They came off the South Platte literally in clouds and provided a major food source for the trout. They were the kind of hatches that could go on for the better part of the day, any day of the year, even in the middle of winter. The trout responded in force with what I came to recognize as a characteristic, head to tail, porpoising kind of rise.

Other anglers like Neil Luehring, John Gierach, Kent Brekke, Bruce

Stagg, and A. K. Best began to notice some quirks that seemed to apply just to the Platte below Cheeseman Reservoir. Along with the midges, it seemed like the only mayfly hatches were Blue-Winged Olives and their *Baetis* relatives and the small mayfly some know as the Tiny White-Winged Black or more scientifically as *Tricorythodes*. We also ran into the lighter colored and somewhat larger Pale Morning Duns (*Ephemerella infrequens*), but they tended to occur a little farther downstream from the dam than the Blue-Winged Olives.

Other anglers, who'd been lucky enough to fish up in Montana, couldn't figure out why their big stonefly nymph imitations had so little effect on the South Platte trout. Stonefly imitations that had brought trout screaming out from under the cutbanks had extremely sporadic, if any, effect on the South Platte trout.

SCUD FISHING IN TAILWATERS

We all agreed on how important the "shrimp" were on the river, to the point that fishing freshwater shrimp or scud patterns every spring became a ritual. The first imitation I ever saw of a freshwater crustacean (genus *Gammarus*) was known as Des's Shrimp and was tied specifically for the South Platte. It was a coppery-colored fly that knocked the trout out when the water was up in the springtime. The funny thing about scuds is that none of us had ever noticed them outside of fishing lakes. I'd heard about them before from a fly fisherman from Pennsylvania who'd fished the wonderful spring creeks there.

I still remember my first encounter with scuds and scud fishing. It was springtime and they were letting some water out of Cheeseman Dam, probably because they'd stored all they needed. I'd come to dread the high water on the river because it meant that I couldn't sight-fish to the trout. Besides, I had trouble getting the fish to strike the "usuals." I was spending a lot of time roaming up and down the bank, which I now know is the first symptom to appear when a skunking is imminent. I came around a bend and saw this guy just hauling in trout hand over fist. He literally couldn't get them off the hook fast enough before he had another one on, and they were all coming from the same run. A couple of the rainbow trout that he caught and released were bigger than any I'd ever seen come out of the river.

After a while, when I couldn't stand it anymore, I walked over to the guy and asked the age-old angler's question. I wanted to know what he was using. He handed me a fly that had been tied on a short-shank hook that appeared from the size of the gap to be about a #16.

"That'll do it. The shrimp get washed out of the weeds this time of year. Trout love it," he said.

I caught trout until I finally broke the fly off. Later, I ran into a friend of mine who'd seen me on the river earlier. He said, "I see you met Des. You know you can buy those flies down at Deckers."

Deckers is a small town along the river. I hopped into my car and drove straight to the general store and came out with a handful of flies.

The one mystery I've never quite figured out about the scuds is why the coppery, pink, or even reddish-colored patterns work so well. I do know that while the live scud is often olive or even gray in color, dead scuds taken from the stomachs of trout or found streamside are actually reddish orange. Some anglers think that the shrimp molt and when they do they turn this orange color. The more cynical ones say that maybe the trout are taking the orange-colored scud imitations for eggs and not scuds at all! It could be true, too, at least on the South Platte, because the best scud fishing occurs in the spring when the rainbows are making their spawning run. Somehow, I still cling to the idea that the trout really do think my orange patterns are scuds. Maybe I'm just naive.

THE INSECTS

As time went by our group noted that the quirks we observed on the South Platte began to add up. Even more importantly, we began to notice that what we'd seen in Cheeseman Canyon seemed to apply, at least in general, to the other bottom-release tailwaters we fished in the West. Our observations were the kind that many anglers are inclined to make. Although we might have written them down in our logs, they were still sightings in the most general sense.

Broken down into major insect groups, they indicated that the larger species of stoneflies didn't seem to exist in the tailwaters we were fishing, particularly near the dam, but smaller species might or might not have been present. We noted that the mayfly species we saw were small near the dams on the tailwaters, which translated into lots of Blue-Winged Olives, but as you moved downstream you saw larger-size species. We couldn't make a lot of sense out of the caddisfly species other than the belief held by some that the caddisflies were a little less common very close to the dams than they were a mile or two downstream. Of course, it wasn't hard to notice that midges occurred in astronomical numbers and that the scuds were also very common, especially the closer you got to the dam.

About this time the rumor began to circulate, as rumors so often do in cults, that there existed a somewhat esoteric sounding doctoral dissertation that addressed the very discoveries we had been making in our what-fly-should-I-put-on-next sort of way on the South Platte. The story was that the dissertation had been written by a student at the University of Colorado and a copy of it was supposed to be in the library stacks, but that it had disappeared mysteriously. It seems as if other fly fishermen had gotten in on the secret, too.

The title was "An Ecological Study of the South Platte River below Cheeseman Reservoir, Colorado with Special Reference to Microinvertebrate Populations as a Function of the Distance from the Reservoir Outlet." It was a Ph.D. thesis by J. V. Ward dated 1973.

I never did get ahold of the thesis itself, but while talking to another professor at the University of Colorado, Jay Windell, the subject of the lack of big stoneflies in the tailwater below Cheeseman Reservoir came up. Dr. Windell said, yes, there appeared to be a relationship to it all but he wasn't the person to talk to. He said I should contact a former student of his by the name of, you guessed it, J. V. Ward. He said that Ward had graduated and taken a position at Colorado State University.

As it turned out Ward and other researchers had been busy for more than a decade documenting the changes that take place in trout habitat when a dam is built across a river. Of particular interest to the scientists, at least initially, were the bottom-release or deep-release dams.

Ward's study of the South Platte in 1973 and subsequent years is an example of the kind of work that has been and is being conducted on

Fly Fishing the Tailwaters

Anglers who seined tailwaters found that the aquatic insect populations were different from those found in unregulated rivers of similar size.

tailwaters throughout the country and the world. Ward set up four sampling stations below the dam. The first one was just a quarter of a kilometer downstream from the dam; the next three were placed at 2.4, 5.0, and 8.5 kilometers below the dam.

Along with the bugs, Ward took a look at the chemistry of the tailwater. Although water chemistry can get a bit complicated from an angler's point of view, the most significant findings below Cheeseman Reservoir were that the waters were quite alkaline and that there wasn't much free carbon dioxide. This means there are plants in the stream that use the carbon dioxide during photosynthesis.

The results of the insect surveys were particularly interesting. What he found was that while the river had fewer species of insects and other aquatic trout foods than an unregulated river might have, the species that it did have occurred in *tremendous* quantities. Although from an ecological viewpoint, which emphasizes that species diversity helps to stabilize a system, the South Platte might have seemed impoverished, from the trout's point of view it was ecstasy, at least if they didn't mind the lack of variety. In other words, there was plenty to eat below the dam!

Professor Ward's findings at his various sampling stations were similar to what the rock-turning fly fishermen had come up with. He noted high densities of midges, an abundance of Blue-Winged Olives and Pale Morning Duns with fewer numbers of *Tricorythodes*. He didn't find any large species of stoneflies but did identify one species of smaller stonefly. Caddisflies were found throughout the study area. He also found scuds (*Gammarus lacustris*) throughout the study area. At the time, we hadn't discovered the real significance of certain species of aquatic worms to tailwater fly fishermen, but Ward's studies did indicate they occurred in significant numbers in the South Platte.

From Ward's work it appeared that the river immediately below the dam contained somewhat lower densities of insects and trout-food species than at the sampling stations a bit farther downstream. His work and that of others seems to indicate that densities increase for a given distance below a dam, then at some point decrease with a concurrent increase in the number of different species of insects.

In effect, the farther you move downstream from the dam the closer the river resembles an unregulated river in terms of the bugs. Put in the most simple terms, that means that as you move farther downstream you'll find a greater variety of insect species, but they'll occur in lower densities. There will also be a lower overall density of bug life.

By now you're probably beginning to think this sounds a little bit like some B-grade movie with a title something like "South Platte Ed and the River of Gloom." Sure bugs are fun, but what about fishing? The point is that once you've picked up a few basic ideas about the biological similarities of many tailwaters, you'll be in a position to go to many of the tailwaters in the country and have a pretty good handle on what you need to do to catch trout.

AQUATIC WORMS

A curious aspect of the uniform flow rates characteristic of bottom-release dams, which has proven to be of significant importance to tail-water anglers, is that they often allow for the colonization of the river by aquatic earthworms of the family *Lumbricidae*. These are what many anglers refer to as San Juan worms.

I first heard about the worms in the early 1970s from, appropriately enough, a San Juan River fly fisherman. He didn't really know what the worms were but he did know that a fly, commonly called a Burlap Fly, was catching trout down on the river. The fly, which is used to imitate cranefly larvae, was quite simple, consisting of a long-shank hook that was wrapped with a strand of burlap for the body. The fly was then hackled fore and aft or sometimes palmered in brown. The fly looked surprisingly like a worm, but I don't think that was what it was tied to imitate at that time.

Within a few years, I believe most San Juan River fly fishermen realized that their river was indeed inhabited in great abundance by aquatic worms and that these worms were a major source of food for the trout there. All kinds of imitations began to appear that ranged from Woolly Worm designs to outlandish "wiggle" patterns that took thirty minutes to tie. The simple fact was that a piece of Ultra Chenille in red or orange tied to a hook worked as well as any.

I fished the San Juan quite often when I lived in the Durango, Colorado area and I don't think the importance of the aquatic worm on that river can be overemphasized. When the word began to get out, the idea of tying imitations of aquatic worms was not met with universal approval in the fly fishing community. It seems that worms had somehow gotten a bad name. I think a fishing pal of mine hit it on the head when he said, "It just pisses them off that you can catch trout, I mean really big trout, on a fly that a five-year-old can tie in twenty seconds."

The most recent development in the San Juan worm story is its increasing use in other tailwaters throughout the United States. When I used to fish the worm imitations on the San Juan River I just assumed the worm was a local phenomenon that occurred in a specific tailwater. I don't remember if I even tried the worm when I traveled to other tailwaters but you can bet if I'd studied Professor Ward's research a little more closely I would have.

As it turns out the San Juan worm imitations have found their way to a number of rivers. A light tan imitation is quite effective at my old stomping grounds on the South Platte River and the word is that the worm is so effective on the Bighorn up in Montana that some people want to outlaw it. Anyway, these aquatic worms are something you might want to keep in mind when fishing tailwaters that have the kind of seasonal constancy in flow rates that they require to survive.

HYDROELECTRIC TAILWATER INSECTS

The trout foods found in the tailwaters below hydroelectric dams are up against several factors that those found in water-storage reservoir tailwaters are not. The most important of these is the occurrence of short-term fluctuations in the flow rates of water releases. The bottom line on how the insects *and* the trout will fare depends on how often and how much the river fluctuates. The shape of the river's channel can also be a factor. A straight channel directly below the dam is more likely to magnify the effect of discharges than, say, a channel that features a prominent stilling basin, bends, braids, or other sources of deflection.

Although it may be hard to believe, it appears that in some hydroelectric tailwaters where the flow fluctuations aren't too extreme the

Fly Fishing the Tailwaters

bugs make out okay. It could be that while the abrupt changes in flow rates aren't optimal for the critters, they aren't a whole lot worse than springtime blowouts that occur during heavy runoff or rains on many unregulated rivers. The actual environment in which many aquatic insects live is the inch or two of relatively "dead" or still water that occurs just off the stream bottom. The fact remains, however, that the nymphal forms of insects that have the ability to migrate from areas that are flooded one day and dry the next have an advantage.

It is interesting to note that in several studies certain stonefly nymphs appear to be the most active migrators. It also seems logical that nymphal forms of insects that cling to streambed surfaces adapt best to the fluctuations common in hydroelectric tailwaters.

Studies show that midges adapt the best even in hydroelectric tailwaters where flow rate fluctuations are extreme. Apparently, they are able to endure longer periods of exposure when stranded in dry areas than other aquatic insect species. Freshwater shrimp or scuds also appear to hold their own in the rapidly fluctuating tailwater flows below many power-generating dams. Although the fluctuations may alter aquatic vegetation that is important scud habitat, these crustaceans are good swimmers that seem able to handle the abrupt changes in flow. It appears that for many species of freshwater shrimp, their preference for somewhat higher water alkalinity may be more of a determining factor to their tailwater populations than the sometimes severe fluctuations in water flow rates below hydroelectric facilities.

The Green River, as it flows at this writing, below the Flaming Gorge Reservoir in Utah is a good example of a benign hydroelectric tailwater. The key to understanding the Green is the realization that the facility is not called upon to generate electricity all the time but acts as a backup during peak periods or when equipment is down at other generating stations. What this means is that water flow rates may stay down at the optimum fishing levels of one thousand to fifteen hundred cubic feet per second (cfs) for long periods of time depending on power requirements.

These longer periods of time between power generation give various algae and aquatic plants the time necessary to gain a foothold in the river. These plants in turn provide habitat for a sizable population of scuds. These scuds are a factor, at times, for anglers fishing the Green.

Tailwater flow rates below water-storage reservoirs tend to be more constant. Constant flows promote aquatic vegetation and more stable stream banks, which in turn promote streamside vegetation.

In terms of mayflies, at least from an angler's point of view, the Green actually is quite similar to what you'd find in a river below a water-storage dam. Blue-Winged Olives (both *Baetis* and the similar but smaller *Pseudocloeon*—all Blue-Winged Olives in my book) and Pale Morning Duns dominate. Caddisflies are present, but as is often the case with caddisflies in tailwaters, their emergence is hard to figure.

Dennis Breer, a longtime fly fisherman and guide on the Green, says that caddisflies on the Green have had their ups and downs over the years. He says he remembers years when the water was a little higher than usual on the Green and the caddis was a prominent insect on the river. The Elk Hair Caddis was the fly to have then. Once again—the caddis are unpredictable.

What is patently predictable on the Green is, you guessed it, the midges.

"I know these fish are getting fat on midges," Breer said. "If you look at their stomach contents you'll find a couple of scuds or this and that, but mainly you'll just see tons and tons of the little stuff."

Dennis can tell you some stories that will absolutely turn you into a believer when it comes to midges on the Green. He told me about the time he was walking the river right after the water had receded a little. A characteristic of the Green is the formation of "scum lines" in the backwaters and along some of the edges. A major component of these lines is the countless shucks from emerging midges. Breer saw a collection of shucks that had been caught in a scum line and had settled on the bank. He figured the line was a foot or a foot and a half wide and a couple of inches thick. It ran for "yards and yards" in Dennis's words. If you figure that your average midge imitation is about a #20 or #22, that collection of shucks that Breer saw on just that portion of the river probably numbered in the millions. The point here is don't forget the midge box when you go out to fish the tailwaters!

The Green also has a sizable component of land-based insects that end up in the river and consequently become trout food. Ants, hoppers and cicadas are seasonally prominent and important. While I think that tailwaters generally tend to promote the occurrence of terrestrials, I have to believe that in the specific case of hoppers and the Green, the river's location out there in the desert country of northeast Utah has something to do with it—that's hopper country for sure.

So, in a lot of ways the Green follows many of the general rules of water-storage tailwaters. Midges are dominant and scuds are also present. The mayfly species tend to be Blue-Winged Olives and Pale Morning Duns, with a tendency for the smaller Blue-Winged Olives to occur closer to the dam. Aquatic worms are also a factor in the Green.

While some generalizations do apply, it's important to note that like all rivers the Green has its share of quirks when it comes to the bugs and the trout. The most interesting quirk on the Green is the craneflies. These flies belong to the same family as the midges, but the similarities stop when you compare sizes. Midges are tiny, whereas the adult, flying forms of craneflies tend to be quite large—on the Green some anglers tie imitations up to #2s on a 4X-long hook for the late-August hatch. The nymphal form of the cranefly is long and wormlike but fatter than the aquatic worms that the San Juan worm is tied to imitate. A simple pattern that is popular on the South Platte River, which also has sizable cranefly populations, is the Rubber Band Fly, and it's as simple to tie as winding a rubber band around the shank of a hook.

Actually, cranefly larvae are more common in many tailwaters than you might think and it pays to keep a few imitations in your nymph box if just for those times, especially in the springtime when nothing else is turning the trick. The unique aspect of Green River craneflies is the fairly predictable hatch of adults that the trout go nuts about. These huge insects in their adult form are poor flyers that are easy prey for the trout. Fishing the hatch, which is often done after dark, can be a scream for anglers using big skater type patterns or more sophisticated match-the-hatch numbers.

Okay, so the Green's a great place when they aren't generating electricity—what happens when they open up the gates? First of all, you can expect little or no warning. So if you happen to have waded across the river to where you saw a few fish rising, you could be out of luck on getting back. Breer has seen the water come up as much as a foot in five minutes. On the Green the water flow rate will increase to approximately 4,000 cfs for maximum power generation. That translates to about a four-foot rise in the water.

This rise will blow out the algae and aquatic vegetation that has grown in the river since the last big release. The chunks of floating debris will tend to muck things up for a few days and make any kind of fishing tough. Breer says he has seen the river's water "pureed" to a moss green on occasion. Along with putting the trout down, the releases can devastate aquatic insect habitat, particularly for those species that depend on the aquatic vegetation for cover and sustenance.

All of this may sound pretty disastrous, and it is in a sense, but I'll tell you why I call it benign. First of all, the water levels aren't rapidly altered or "bounced" very often. When they are bounced, they generally don't stay at high levels for more than five or six days. Secondly, the Green might best be considered a floater's river. The floating fly fisherman, even during periods of high water, might be able to find a few midging trout in the back eddies or he could nymph the bottom of the streambed, right down the middle, where the trout tend to lie during the periods of high water. The floating fly fisherman is also relatively safe when water levels rise abruptly as compared to wading anglers, who can experience real danger. Finally, the Green cleans up within a day or so after water levels stabilize, and the trout have been known to feed heavily at those times.

Really, the Green is a model tailwater when it comes to anglers' complaints. Anglers always complain that when water levels are changed they are changed too quickly and that, while they can live with either high or low water, the continual bouncing of water levels is difficult for them to handle—not to mention the effect it has on the trout and their food sources.

Dennis hit it on the head one afternoon when he said, "This is a very typical tailwater fishery and there are times when they blow that water out and there isn't a thing in the world you can do about it."

I agree with him. One of the hardest things to get used to as a tailwater fly fisherman is to experience ecstasy one day on the river, say when there's a six-hour-long Pale Morning Dun hatch, then go home and call all your pals to tell them the good news and that they just *have* to go fishing the very next day. After they hear the excitement in your voice they'll do anything to get off work the next day: they postpone weddings, put off heavy financial deals, beg friends to drive the kids to school—all because the hatch is on.

For the entire trip up to the river you sit in the backseat of the car raving about how good it was the day before and watch them salivate. It can get very ugly when you drive around the final bend and everyone notices the water has come up 400 percent and the "cosmic" hatch has been blown down the river twenty-seven miles.

The Smith River in southern Virginia is an example of a more extreme kind of hydroelectric tailwater fishery. The Smith is on the far eastern end of a swath of hydroelectric tailwater trout fisheries that occur from Missouri to Arkansas to Tennessee to Kentucky and just barely slide into Virginia. The cold waters released from these reservoirs have created trout fisheries in some places where they never existed or transformed simple put-and-take waters into trophy-trout water.

The Smith and the rivers like it are characterized by abrupt changes in flow rates when power is generated. A common pattern for flows on these rivers is maximum discharge during the daytime hours with lowered rates during the night. In many cases power is not generated during the weekends. This is the case on the Smith.

One difference in the bug life of the Smith is that scuds are not a factor because the water is not alkaline enough to support them. The constant scouring of the channel by the short-term water fluctuations used in generating the electricity leaves little time for any aquatic vegetation to grab hold in the river. That's the down side. The up side is that the discharges have also scoured out the silt deposits that can be common in this part of the country.

Once again, the great survivors are the midges, which occur in tremendous numbers. Surprisingly, mayflies are also important on the Smith. The Blue-Winged Olives, *Tricorythodes*, and the Sulphurs, which I see as an eastern equivalent of the western Pale Morning Dun, seem to do the best. Farther downstream from the dam an unusual jet-black caddis is common enough, especially in the springtime, to be on the trout's menu. The river also supports both sculpin and minnow populations.

What all of this should tell you is how resilient both the insect and trout populations can be even in more extreme tailwater environments. The insect populations point out a basic tailwater axiom that appears to be supported by Professor Ward's work. It seems that although most tailwater systems have fewer species of insects, the species that occur do so in large numbers. From an angler's point of view this means that certain groups of fly patterns can be tremendously important while other patterns, which often hold places of honor in the fly box, are of less value.

Since the Smith is not much of a floater's river, anglers end up restricting their activities to periods of low water-flow rates. This means constant calls to ascertain the power-generating schedule. Water fluctuations are so extreme that horns are sounded to warn anyone in the river channel that discharges are imminent and that they should reel in immediately and leave.

The reason all the brouhaha over flow rates doesn't deter fishermen is obvious when you look at some of the brown trout that live in the Smith. In one three-mile section where special regulations are in effect, trout in the 4-pound to 8-pound range have been caught, and 16-inchers to 18-inchers aren't uncommon. All this is happening in an area not known historically for big trout. In the stilling basins directly below the dam, monster brown trout up to 18 pounds gorge on threadfin shad that are sucked into the turbines and ground up. Although these browns are more commonly the prey of bait fishermen, it is tempting to rig up some sort of chum fly, maybe something similar to the kind of pattern fly fishermen use for bluefish, and go after them with the fly rod. Anyway, the Smith is an example of a tailwater with highly fluctuating waters that still maintains good populations of quality trout food as well as the trout to eat it.

INSECTS ON MIXED TAILWATERS

If you want to throw a wrench into all of this, take a moment to consider the tailwaters with mixing towers or those that have multiple gates so that the temperature of the water released can be varied. Most often this means that the very cold waters common in bottom-release dams can be moderated and warmed up a bit. Many of the newer dams are capable of mixing water, and a few older ones, like Flaming Gorge Dam on the Green River, have been retrofitted with water-mixing devices.

I don't think the difference in water temperatures in these mixed tailwaters has changed the species of bugs that you find in the river as much as *where* you might find them. This is true for the trout, too. On the Green

River, before the mixing boxes were installed, the lower sections of the river were home to some very large rainbow trout. This occurred because the fish sought out water farther downstream that had been warmed by the sun and air temperature. Now, with the warmer, mixed water coming out of the dam, the optimal water temperature for the rainbow trout is found upstream closer to the dam. Brown trout, which have a higher tolerance to warmer water temperatures, have come into the even warmer, lower sections of the river that once held rainbows.

I also think that insect species that require cooler water temperatures may now also have migrated to sections closer to the dam. If anything, you should keep your eyes open to the possibility of finding a few more species of mayflies (possibly even the larger mayfly species) in these warmer mixed waters.

TAILWATER STONEFLIES

The McPhee Dam on the Dolores River in southwestern Colorado was completed in the early 1980s and features a multi-gate design. Although this tailwater, which occurs below a water-storage reservoir, is typical in that it harbors large numbers of midges, the mayflies common to tailwaters, and a sizable caddisfly population, it differs in one important aspect. There is a significant population of golden stoneflies.

Researchers believe that the larger species of stoneflies that are so important on many unregulated rivers and on some regulated rivers are absent from many bottom-release tailwaters because of low water temperatures. It appears that in order for the immature stoneflies to develop, certain "cues" in water temperature are needed. The most generally held opinion is that a certain minimum amount of thermal energy—or "degree days" as the biologists say—is necessary for the stoneflies to hatch.

What this means is, as a tailwater fly fisherman, you have to be careful about making any all-encompassing conclusions about the big stoneflies. You may fish any number of deep-release tailwaters where the giant stonefly species are absent altogether. But then again you may find yourself in the Box Canyon below the Island Park Reservoir on the Henry's Fork of the Snake River. It is saturated with the big stones.

Over time, the reasons why the giant stoneflies appear in some tailwaters but not in others will become translucent to you; however, it will never be absolutely clear.

The Henry's Fork is fairly easy to explain—the reservoir above the canyon is pretty shallow and water releases are relatively warm. Actually, even though there is a dam on the Henry's Fork, it's difficult to think about it as a *real* tailwater because of the geothermal activity and springs that influence it. It's difficult to see much of a tailwater profile there at all.

Other tailwaters that harbor good populations of big stoneflies like the Madison below Hebgen Reservoir and the South Fork of the Snake are more obscure. It works down to a combination of many factors. The big *Pteronarcys* stoneflies thrive on large-size detritus. If none is coming through the dam and temperature and oxygen content are borderline, their populations may diminish. Some of the bigger yellow or golden stoneflies are predators, and if the bugs they like to eat don't occur below a dam for whatever reason, you may not find them there, either.

I've fished many tailwaters where the big stones are simply not a factor. In some cases the stoneflies were never a factor in these rivers even before the dam was constructed. In other cases they might have been marginal at best and the tailwater took away their survival edge. Where strong populations of the big stones did occur and a deep-release dam was constructed, what you'll find is a decrease in populations directly below the dam where the water is very cold. As you move farther downstream where the water is warmer, populations rebound strongly.

The lesson to learn from the stoneflies in relation to tailwaters is that conditions for all insects change as the water moves downstream. As an angler you occasionally need to turn over some rocks and sample the drifting insects to stay on top of things. Be careful about coming to any conclusions about the entire tailwater based on fishing just one section.

So, in the case of stoneflies in tailwaters, you'd better not leave all your imitations at home even though in an *overall* sense they may be less significant below the dams on some tailwaters. You certainly don't ever want to go to Montana or the Yellowstone area without big stonefly imitations no matter where you plan to fish (although there will be tailwaters, like the Missouri or Bighorn, where you won't find many of the big species). If the tailwater you intend to fish has warmer water, better pack your stoneflies, too. Best of all, just call ahead to a fly shop on the tailwater you plan to fish and ask them if there are big stones in *their* river or not, and forget about science and logic altogether!

A TAILWATER TROUT MENU

So here's what we know: The water released into many tailwaters has a more limited range in temperature, staying warmer in the winter and cooler in the summer. This difference in temperature variation, along with changes in water chemistry and possibly the streambed itself, causes some trout food populations to decrease while others increase.

As a general rule, tailwater fly fishermen need to concentrate their fly-tying efforts on patterns that include midges, smaller-size mayflies, scuds, and in some cases aquatic worm patterns. Caddisfly patterns may be tremendously significant in some fisheries and not very productive at all in others. The importance of giant stonefly species may be diminished in some tailwaters, particularly directly below the dam, but smaller-size species may be unaffected. Terrestrial insects may have added importance to tailwater fly fishermen in some situations. Different conditions dictated by different types of tailwaters may alter the kinds of foods available to trout.

By concentrating on several critically important groups of trout foods and by using suitable techniques, fly fishermen have a very good chance of successfully fishing any number of tailwaters throughout the country.

Baitfish like this sculpin are found in some tailwaters.

Useful equipment for tailwater fly fishermen includes (from right to left) rod and reel, fly fishing vest and landing net, collapsible wading staff, camera, stocking-foot neoprene waders with gravel guards and wading shoes, heavy socks, wading cleats, additional fly rods, and a heavy sweater.

CHAPTER 3

Accouterments

IT SEEMS THAT fly fishermen, as a group, don't need much encouragement when it comes to acquiring the tools of their trade. As much as any sport, fly fishing is a sport of minutiae and nowhere is this more apparent than in the specialized world of the tailwater angler. The accouterments of the fly fisherman are at their seductive best when they not only perform the job they were designed to do, but are also pleasing to the eye and have that perfect heft in the hand.

There *is* a practical side to the aesthetics of fine tackle, too. I don't know how many times the simple act of uncasing a rod or reel, or the opening of a particular fly box, has pulled me through a long winter's night. Sometimes just assembling a favorite rod and waggling it around a little can bring back memories of trout brought to net and fantasies of the trout yet to come.

Besides all the art, beauty, and memories that go with your "stuff," it can serve as an emotional backup for those particularly tough days astream. You can always get into how wonderful your equipment is when you're getting skunked on your favorite tailwater. You might laugh, but I assure you it has been done.

FLY RODS

Of all the equipment fly fishermen use, they probably agonize the most over fly rods. This is as it should be because the fly rod is probably the most important, if not the most expensive, investment that an angler makes. If you've ever needed an excuse to carry two or three fly rods when you go fishing you will be well served as a tailwater fly fisherman. Depending on the river, figure on the faster action of a graphite rod for nymphing and possibly some streamer work. This rod *could* actually double for the dry-fly rod and maybe even for delicate midge work, but it is a sweet pleasure indeed to have a cherished split cane rod available when things happen on the water's surface.

The business of deciding on an appropriate fly rod has gotten increasingly complex over the past several decades. I still remember the simplicity of it all when I got my first decent-casting fly rod. A few had come before it, but they were the kind of catastrophes that now are difficult to find, which brings up one of the advantages of the ever increasing interest in fly fishing—it's pretty hard to buy a new fly rod nowadays that is completely worthless when it comes to casting.

Anyway, my first good rod was a fiberglass number manufactured by Cortland. It came in a beginner's set with matching reel and line. This rod had an action that was considered just a hair slower than fast in its day. By today's standards, with all the lightning-quick graphites available, it would probably be considered a moderate action. The point is that the rod performed just fine. It was fast enough to nymph with and it cast delicately enough for dry fly and even midging situations. I still have the rod, although I must say it's just collected dust over the past fifteen years. But I *could* use it tomorrow and probably, with the exception of very long casting situations, catch as many trout with it as with any of the other dozen or so rods I have.

What it boils down to is that what *you* are really going to need in a fly rod is pretty subjective. For modern fly fishers, aside from matching the rod to the situations in which it will most often be fished, it's not so much a question of which fly rod they can get by with, but more one of what rod they would prefer to take fishing with them. A fine fly rod very quickly can become a companion and friend. With that in mind let's have a look at graphite. There has been no compound or synthetic formulation since nylon replaced silk as the material of choice in fly lines that has had a more profound effect on fly fishing. Although fiberglass fly rods are still obtainable, they get harder to find every season. Graphite has, for all practical purposes, replaced fiberglass as the standard material for the construction of production fly rods.

Graphite rods initially started out as the "next step up" from fiberglass. They required more of an economic commitment on the angler's part but

Fly Fishing the Tailwaters

demonstrated a pronounced difference in casting performance. This was particularly apparent in the distance department. Even with the earliest graphite rods, which amounted to little more than prototypes, an average caster could figure on a 15 to 20 percent increase in casting distance.

The explosion in graphite rod technology over the past decade is obvious to anyone who has tried to buy a fly rod. It seems like what used to be a pleasant afternoon spent casting demonstration rods down at the neighborhood fly shop has, in some cases, turned into a super-charged high-tech experience. I'm half scared to go near the fly rods anymore for fear that some kid will pounce on me and start raving about high-performance, high-modulus graphite, and the latest Stealth technology available in fly rods.

The simple fact is that I gave up trying to understand what goes into the engineering of a graphite fly rod ten years ago. I still decide whether I like a rod the old way: I cast it. It's that simple. Take the rod outside with the correct weight double-taper line and give it a whirl. If you like it, try casting with a weight-forward line one size heavier than the double-taper and see what you think. After that you might want to try lighter or heavier line weights just to see what the rod does and how it feels. Cast the rod at both short and long distances. Try casting into the wind and with the wind behind you, then go home and sleep on it. When it comes time for the big purchase, buy the rod that you liked casting the most and forget about what the kid with the engineering degree told you.

I could say that when it comes to specific line weights and rod lengths the rod should be matched to the predominant fishing conditions you expect to encounter and to some degree the fishing techniques you will employ, and for the most part I'd probably be right. The fact is, though, that graphite gives you a lot of latitude, particularly if you like going light. I know any number of anglers who do just fine on the big western tailwaters with 5-weight or even 4-weight graphite rods in the longer lengths. The higher line speeds obtainable with the graphite materials even allow these lighter lines to be cast into some pretty strong head winds.

I don't really want to recommend a specific "tailwater" fly rod but I wouldn't feel bad about relating a personal bias or two. First of all, I think the longer rods in the 8 1/2-foot or better yet 9-foot lengths are best. The longer rod lengths, which are technically difficult to produce with some materials, can be made easily from graphite. Not only is the graphite lightweight but it is quite strong, too. This means butt diameters can be absurdly small. Hence, overall rod weights in the longer graphite rods are significantly lighter when compared to other rod-building materials. The extra rod length is an advantage for fly fishing many tailwaters where nymphing is an important technique and where the extra length and reach is necessary for mending line. I look for faster action in a tailwater fly rod both for quicker response when nymphing and for increased line speed when casting in windy conditions.

Actually, the action in graphite rods is almost academic nowadays since most can be considered moderately fast or just plain fast. There was a time when rod makers toyed with slower actions in graphite that even approached those of bamboo rods, but angler response was not good. It seems like a fast tip is associated with graphite by anglers and if they want a slower, more sensitive rod they look to cane or fiberglass.

So, what if you held me up against the wall and demanded to know *the* tailwater graphite fly rod? Sure, I'd say a 6-weight at 9 feet—but you'd have to beat it out of me. I have a 5-weight at 9 feet I'm rather fond of, too.

Speaking of cane rods, don't relegate yours to the closet just because you're heading out for a little tailwater angling. There is certainly a place for the venerable bamboo rod on tailwaters and there are anglers who fish nothing but cane on their favorite tailwaters. I fished the South Platte for a number of years with a fine little 7 1/2-foot cane rod for a 5-weight line built by Gil Lipp. It was just barely adequate for nymphing, but I was willing to overlook that for the ecstasy of fishing the midge hatches with such a responsive rod.

I think that's the way to look at cane when it comes to fly fishing the tailwaters, too. It's as much a matter of how you see yourself as anything. If you are predominantly a dry-fly fisherman who fishes nymphs just to get from one hatch to the next it would be a crime not to have the cane rod along. Actually, I've seen a bit of a revival in the cane rods over the past few years. I think it has a lot to do with the quality of rods being built by the custom rod builders around the country now. These rods feel right in the hand and have a bit of quickness to them. To my mind there is no better way to fish the rise.

My friend A. K. Best, who is an almost fanatical devotee of cane rods, once put it this way when we were in a fly fishing store looking at rods. A young clerk had just finished telling us that a certain graphite rod could "cast the line as straight as an arrow." A. K. replied, "I don't want to cast a straight line. I want to throw slack and curves. I need to get good, long drifts. Damn plastic rods are all the same." That was straight from the heart of the best dry-fly fisherman I know.

FLY REELS

When it comes to reels for fly rods I don't necessarily agree with the opinion that a fly reel is just a place to store the fly line. When purchasing a fly reel several considerations must be made. First, I think a reel must be matched to your rod in terms of weight and balance. This is best accomplished in consultation with your local fly shop or by following the rod manufacturer's recommendations. It's my belief that as a tailwater fly fisherman you will probably be exposed to more and larger trout than you are used to catching on a comparable unregulated river and that you had best be prepared to deal with them. That means adequate backing on your reel and setting things up so that fish can be played from the reel. If you hook into a large fish you will find that a fly reel ceases to be just a place where fly line is stored. Larger fish are best played from the reel, where the fly line and backing can be effectively managed.

I cast right-handed, and since I don't like to switch my rod from my casting hand to my left hand when playing a fish from the reel, I need to have a left-hand retrieve reel. Almost all reels are now designed so they can be switched to either left-hand or right-hand retrieve, but it pays to double-check on that feature particularly on larger models and some English brands.

An exposed-rim reel can be useful in playing larger fish since it can be palmed to produce extra braking and drag. I look for this feature more on the larger capacity reels, although if you desire it on a smaller-size reel there are a number of manufacturers who make it available. Most reels come with some sort of mechanical drag that provides a variety of settings from light to heavy. Some of these drags are good and others are not. The only way to find out is to put a line on the reel and mess around with the various drag settings.

One final word on reels. You do need some sort of minimum standard of quality. I learned that on the Clearwater River in northern Idaho one year when I was fishing for the steelhead that run up to the hatchery below the Dworshak Dam. It isn't an easy run for fly fishers where the average steelhead costs about sixty to seventy angling hours. I had rigged up my heaviest rod with a large old reel I had lying around, figuring that I could use the extra capacity for backing. About four days into the fishing I got the strike I had been working for and the line scorched off the reel on the first run; at least it did until the spool began to wobble and make funny noises. Then it froze and stopped dead. I lost the steelhead *and* my entire fly line when it broke at the knot to the backing.

I've never been sure if the reason that reel seized up was because of poor manufacturing or if maybe I'd bent it just slightly out of true in a fall or by tossing it into the trunk of the car (it was that kind of reel). Whatever the reason, it pays to buy a reel you can depend on, and if you do stumble and fall a lot around rivers like I seem to do, take time to check your equipment and make sure it is still functional.

I don't get too worked up about fly lines when it comes to tailwater fishing and get by just fine with a double-taper in the weight required for my rod. I fished weight-forward tapers for a while but came back to the double-tapers when I figured I could double the line's life by reversing the double-taper when one end wore out. On the bigger tailwaters some fly fishermen swear by Sink-Tip lines for certain nymphing situations, but I just haven't found a need for them.

WADERS

If selecting a rod and a matching reel is sweet agony, then getting a pair of waders that you can live with is just plain agony. Among an angler's toys, waders are *the* weak link. A word to the wise would be that no matter what kind of waders you choose, be sure to buy a repair kit that will fix them.

In the same way that graphite took over the rod-making industry, neoprene has conquered much of the wader market. The other great change has been a switch in style from the clunky boot-foot wader to the stocking-foot wader, which requires a wading shoe.

Although neoprene does have some drawbacks, I still believe that the stocking-foot, neoprene chest wader is the best option for the tailwater angler. The most important reason is the increased mobility that the stocking-foot style affords you. Part of the reason for that increased mobility is that you can get a better fit with the stocking-foot waders because they are available in a variety of sizes depending on your height and girth. The added mobility is the kind of thing that you notice at the end of the day when you just don't seem as tired, or when you go to step up on a rock to get the perfect cast to a trout that's midging on the other side of the channel. Boot-foot waders simply don't cut it when it comes to high stepping.

The reason that you need the neoprene stocking-foot wader rather than any old stocking-foot wader is that it does tend to be warmer. Warmth is something you begin to appreciate as a tailwater fly fisherman. Not only are many tailwaters located at the bottom of deep canyons that get little sunshine, but most are known for cold water—that's why the trout do so well. Water temperatures below some deep-release dams may range between 38 and 44 degrees Fahrenheit. Even a tailwater that's influenced by some sort of water-mixing device can seldom be expected to get above the 50s.

A disadvantage I've found with the neoprene waders is that the seams are still a problem and will most likely leak sooner or later. This can be avoided by a little preseason preventive maintenance—a requirement for all waders, anyway. Pay special attention to seams in the crotch area and at the feet. Another problem, though minor, that I've come across particularly in lined neoprene waders is the tendency for condensation to collect in the heel area. Although this isn't much of a problem, it can lead you to believe you have a leak when in fact there is no leak at all.

The flip side of the warmth that these waders provide in icy waters is that they can get *very* hot in summer fishing conditions, particularly when water is low and you can't immerse yourself any deeper than your ankles. If you have to do any hiking into the river when the weather is hot, it's probably best to carry the neoprene waders and get into them when you reach the river, if just to keep from sweating yourself wet or, more ominously, getting heat stroke.

Many anglers have found that they can obtain some relief from the heat by wetting as much of the outer neoprene wader fabric as possible and waiting for the cooling effect as the water evaporates. It has brought about a new behavioral characteristic among neoprened anglers on hot afternoons—you will see them wallowing around like water buffalo along the edges of the pools and riffles trying to wet down their waders.

There are some alternatives to neoprene that are perfectly serviceable. Many anglers prefer the flyweight nylon stocking-foot waders. These offer the same freedom of movement and are considerably cooler in the summer months. They can also be used in colder weather by simply adding layers of long underwear underneath. Many fly fishermen like the idea that they can just put on the flyweights over their blue jeans or trousers, something difficult to do with neoprene waders where a pair of polypropylene long johns underneath is the rule. Flyweights are also considerably less expensive than neoprenes.

The other stocking-foot option is the old latex standbys. This type was the first stocking-foot wader available and continues to have advocates. They are easy to get into, hold up well, are moderately priced, and are very easy to repair. Like flyweights, extra layers can be added underneath for cold fishing conditions. The drawbacks are that they don't come in many size varieties, so getting a good fit can be difficult, and they can get pretty hot in summer fishing conditions.

A word about wading shoes. Make sure you try them on with the waders and socks you intend to wear with them. Neoprene waders, in particular, are bulky in the foot area and you may need to go up a few sizes in the wading shoe. If you intend to use different types of stocking-foot waders with one pair of wading shoes (for example, neoprene, flyweight, and latex), size the wading shoes for your neoprene waders because they require the biggest shoe. Make sure the shoes are big enough. If they're too tight, expect cold feet.

Wading shoes are made from a variety of materials. The synthetics appear to be the most popular and can be purchased in a range of prices. Pay special attention to the felt soles. I think felts that are sewn and glued on rather than just glued on hold up better. I've never had much luck glu-

Fly Fishing the Tailwaters

ing replacement felts on to old wading shoes, either, so I take them to a shoemaker, who sews and glues on the replacement felts. I personally prefer leather wading shoes. I like the extra support they provide and they simply hold up better than any synthetic I've ever used. The pair I'm using now is three years old and going strong. I just coat them with a waterproofing grease once a year and that's all there is to maintenance. The one disadvantage to leather is that it takes longer to dry than synthetics and is a little heavier.

The other wader options include standard boot-foot waders, which I think are too cumbersome for river fly fishing, and hip waders. Now, hippers do offer some advantages under the right conditions. They offer maximum mobility and are cool in the summer. The disadvantage is obvious—they are only appropriate in low-water situations. Tailwater fly fishermen who use hippers run the added risk that the water level that is wadable in the morning with hippers may go up in the afternoon and become unwadable. Nonetheless, on tailwaters where I know the general schedule of water releases, I often use hippers during periods of low water in the late summer and autumn just because they are so handy.

WADING STAFFS AND SAFETY DEVICES

Since we're on the subject of wading, there are some wading safety devices that can be important to tailwater fly fishermen. A wading staff can be made from almost anything—I have a pal who uses a varnished old stick with a gnarl on the end. For years I used an aluminum ski pole with the basket removed. The most practical wading staff I've found is a tubular aluminum job with sections connected by shock cord. It folds neatly into a leather holster that fits on your wading belt. The staff comes together quickly when removed from the holster and *usually* comes apart quickly for storage. A little paraffin on the joints helps. Whatever kind of staff you choose, it should be attached by a cord to your wading belt or vest so that it can be trailed behind you in the water when you're working a fish. When crossing heavy water, place the staff on your upstream side where you can lean into it, rather than in a less stable downstream position.

The algae and aquatic plant growth that is so characteristic and important in many tailwaters is also responsible for the sometimes treacherous wading conditions. The streambed that provides such good insect habitat because it's covered with a thin layer of algae can seem like a field of greased cannonballs when you're wading.

I would suggest that you don't leave home without the wading staff, particularly if you're headed to unfamiliar waters. It can come in handy for all sorts of chores. I've used mine to get the extra reach necessary to recover an Elk Hair Caddis imitation that I backcast into the streamside foliage. Once, on the Arkansas River, I used it to persuade a rattlesnake that my wading shoe was, in fact, inedible.

I remember getting whambozzled once on the San Juan River. I'd spent the better part of the day just above the Texas Hole on the southern side of the river, which consists of a number of benign braids, backwaters, and channels when the river is at normal levels. Toward afternoon, I wandered over to the main channel on the north side of the river, which is considerably swifter and deeper than the braids. I nymphed for a while along the edge of the faster water, then decided to wade out to work some dead water behind a big rock in the middle of the channel.

The surprise came when I went to turn back to shore. I couldn't do it! The current was strong enough that it scared me to lift a foot and turn. It was the kind of situation where you can feel the sand washing out from under your heels. I stood there for about five or ten minutes trying to figure out my options when another fisherman came along.

"I'm stuck out here. Can't get turned around!" I called out to him.

"Wow, that's too bad," he yelled back and continued downstream without another thought to my predicament. I stood out there for another ten minutes before I finally got up the courage to make the turn and shuffle very quickly, with the current, back to the shore. It was that kind of buoyant, floating shuffle step that wading anglers on the verge of spinning out of control use. I kept my eyes open for the "friendly" angler the rest of the afternoon but never did see him again, which is probably best. If I'd had my wading staff that afternoon I'm sure I wouldn't have had any problems. A pair of wading cleats wouldn't have been a bad idea, either.

Wading cleats are those numbers you see tossed off into the corner down at the fly shop. Most often they look like a pair of rubbers that have aluminum bars or cleats attached to the bottom. You use them by simply pulling them over your wading shoes. The aluminum cleats cut through the algae that often coats the rocks in tailwaters and do a pretty good job at adding some stability to an angler's wading life. Other options for cleats include a tie-on variety with golf-shoe spikes on the bottom. A less severe solution consists of carbide-tipped steel studs that have been glued into replacement felts for the bottom of your wading shoes.

The wading cleats are a pretty extreme measure and I've found that I usually do all right with the wading staff and a good set of felts on my wading shoes, but if you need the cleats, you need them in the worst way. They are relatively cheap insurance especially if you're headed to a tailwater known for treacherous footing.

Like everyone who has fished for any amount of time, I've had my share of dunkings. I've been lucky in that most of mine have been pretty innocuous. They tend to be of the "three-point" variety where I go into the classic football lineman's stance *very* quickly and end up with a wet arm. I've found that I am most likely to fall in the river when I'm wading to or from an area I plan to fish. I think it occurs then because my mind is often not on what I'm doing.

I am fortunate never to have been involved in a life-threatening wading mishap, but you hear about them and anglers are, in fact, lost to wading accidents every season. I have a simple rule of thumb for determining the seriousness of a wading mishap—if an angler lets go of his fly rod consider the situation ugly. I've seen anglers bash through very heavy rapids adamantly refusing to let go of their fishing rods even though they were looking death squarely in the eye. So you see what I mean.

If you are ever surprised by a serious wading mishap, the one bit of advice I've been given that made sense was not to try to "run" along the stream bottom. Once you've lost control you might catch a foot or ankle and the current would then push you under. It is best to get your feet up in the water and out in front of you as protection against rocks and other obstructions in the river. Work your way to shore by using the river currents to your advantage as opposed to fighting them.

Recently, I have seen the introduction of some flotation devices for fly fishermen. The first were full vestlike affairs that inflated Mae West style by pulling a cord. I think most anglers shied away from them simply because of their bulkiness. Of course, standard flotation vests are also too bulky. The latest innovation is an unobtrusive vest that fits over the head and almost looks like a pair of suspenders. It's inflated by a pull cord that activates a carbon dioxide cartridge, or it can be blown up with a mouth tube. It will offer enough flotation to keep an angler's head above water. I've never experimented with any of these devices but they might be a consideration for anglers who fish tailraces where water releases are unpredictable.

FLY FISHING VESTS AND ACCESSORIES

Okay, back to the less perilous things fly fishermen prefer to talk about. What about fly fishing vests? From a tailwater angler's point of view I don't think the style you choose will make any appreciable difference. If you know that you'll be involved in deep wading situations on a regular basis, you might want to consider a "shorty" vest, which will go a long way toward keeping your fly boxes and other doodads dry.

I wouldn't try to tackle the question of what you need *in* your fly vest. Let it suffice to say that I have seen some pretty weird things in fly fishing vests, not to mention the fly fishermen themselves. What goes into your vest is by and large a personal matter, but if you're like me the one thing you can be sure of is that it will be too much.

There are just a few items that I think may be of particular importance in a tailwater fly fisherman's vest. I think you should have some sort of forceps (we always called these hemostats) to be used mainly for removing those hard-to-get-at flies from the trout's mouth. Since many tailwaters do have special regulations where some or all trout must be returned to the water, the less trauma to the fish the better. The forceps can help in those tough cases. They also come in handy when used as a mini-vise for holding a fly that you have chosen to alter in some way to better suit a selective trout's desires.

In that same vein I always carry small fly-tying scissors, with the points well protected, in my vest. I can't count the times I've used them to alter flies *and* cut patches for streamside wader repairs. The little nail clippers that you use to trim leaders just aren't adequate for this more precise type of work.

Pliers of some sort (a good hemostat can sometimes double here) come in handy for crimping down hook barbs if you find yourself in an area that is restricted to the use of barbless hooks. A good hook-sharpening file of the right shape can also be used in a pinch to remove the barb from a hook or two or to touch up a dull hook.

You should also carry a landing net. Most anglers attach them to the D-ring on the back of their vests with some sort of French clip arrangement for easy access. I also have my net attached to the vest with a loop of elastic cord at the D-ring so that I can remove it with the French clip without losing it if I drop it into the river. This setup is also useful if a trout becomes uncooperative when it is in close and you find that both your hands are needed. The net can then simply be dropped into the water where it will trail behind you until needed.

Where catch-and-release regulations are in effect, the landing net should be considered a conservation tool. It helps in landing a trout more quickly, increasing the chances of releasing it in better condition. Some anglers claim that the longer-lasting nylon net bags that come as standard equipment on most landing nets can cut or injure fish and opt to replace them with cotton net bags.

I'm not a fanatic on knowing every bug that's floating down the river but occasionally it *is* crucial to find out exactly what's in the drift. I carry a piece of nylon screening about one foot by two feet folded up in the back of my vest for this purpose. It's light, simple, and gets the job done as well as more elaborate "bug catchers."

Whether you carry them in your vest or wear them all the time, a pair of Polaroid sunglasses is indispensable on the tailwaters. Not only do they protect your eyes from bright conditions, they also cut the glare on the water, making it possible for you to spot trout. Being able to see the trout and what they are doing really helps, especially when nymphing. I also think that this kind of sight-fishing to nymphing trout adds an exciting dimension to the nympher's craft.

The best tint for fly fishing Polaroids that I've found is amber. These lenses are dark enough to reduce brightness, and also provide added contrast, which increases definition. This in turn helps you see the often

A fly fishing vest for tailwater fly fishermen should include forceps for hook removal (left side of vest), a scissors/pliers and leader gauge (right side of vest), and a landing net attached to the back of the vest.

Fly Fishing the Tailwaters

cryptically defined trout as they hug the bottom or the bank on the opposite side of the river. Some anglers use dark Polaroids for bright days but switch to yellow, high-contrast lenses for overcast and stormy weather. I wear prescription glasses and had a pair of amber Photograde Polaroids made. They're excellent in most conditions although they don't quite lighten up enough on the more overcast days. I can't overemphasize how important the Polaroids are to you. Buy them, beg them, borrow them, or steal them—they're a must.

Along the lines of protection, don't forget a hat. I've got an up-downer that I keep in the back of my vest at all times. I may be a little more sensitive than some to the hat issue since I'm protecting a lot more bare territory up there than just a hair part. But I still think you'll feel a lot livelier when that late-evening hatch comes off if you've thought to wear a hat, especially during the heat of the day.

A sunscreen is also very important. I know a number of guides here in the western states who have skin cancers on their hands because they've gotten too much sun over the years. Nymph fishermen especially notice how easy it is to get a sunburn along the inside of the wrist on their rod hand. Don't take the chance. Look for a waterproof sunscreen with a high sun-protection value. Your local pharmacist or a dermatologist can help you when selecting a particular name brand. Try to put on the sunscreen a half hour or hour before you hit the river and reapply as the day progresses and the sun gets higher in the sky. All exposed areas of skin should be covered.

GEAR FOR RAIN AND COLD

For wet-weather protection always carry a rainjacket. The more you fly fish tailwaters the more you'll find that you want to be on the water when it's overcast and raining or drizzling. The very best hatch of Pale Morning Duns that I've ever seen occurred during a rainstorm that alternately went from drizzle to moderately heavy rainfall. This hatch lasted for an entire day and the trout fed voraciously on emergers that were taking longer than usual to get out of their shucks and into the air because of the rain. At times like this you don't want to be cold and wet and cussing the fact that you left your rainjacket at home. Put the rainjacket in the back of your vest and leave it there, no matter what the weather forecast is. The rainjacket can also serve double duty as windbreaker and can even help to offset the effects of a cool evening on the river if you've forgotten your sweater.

When temperatures are cold always assume that the tailwaters associated with the deeper river canyons will be colder than you think. Shorter periods of daytime sunshine and the tendency for colder air to sink into the canyon bottoms can be the makings of an unpleasant surprise for unprepared anglers. Carrying a wool or lightweight pile sweater in all but the warmest weather is wise. I would also suggest that you put a pair of gloves in the back pocket of your fly fishing vest. I'm a bit old-fashioned and still use the fingerless wool gloves once favored by rock climbers, but it appears that neoprene has taken over the fishing-glove market as well as the wader market.

That may sound like a lot to stuff into the back of your fly fishing vest and I admit it is. But it *will* fit if you watch your p's and q's. You can always employ the services of a small pack if you need to bring additional equipment or, more likely, clothing, say for a winter fishing foray, to the river.

A final point...don't forget lunch!

A landing net should be considered a conservation tool. The Polaroid sunglasses are a must for spotting fish.

Accouterments

Aquatic worms, sometimes referred to as San Juan worms, are plentiful in a number of tailwaters. They are best fished using dead drift tactics.

CHAPTER 4

The Nympher's Art
and Other
Deep-Water Diversions

A STANDARD SAYING AMONG fly fishermen is that trout spend anywhere from 80 to 90 percent of their time feeding below the water's surface on the immature forms of aquatic insects. Some anglers are even more precise, but whatever the exact percentage is, it's safe to say that to fully appreciate any tailwater fishery you will have to learn the fine art of nymphing. You can figure that a good nympher will consistently take more and larger trout. The skills required, though, are hard earned and involve learning to find fish, fly selection, inspired concentration, and a measure of good humor.

I have a notion that nymphing techniques are even more productive in tailwater fisheries than in equivalent free-flowing rivers. I say this because of a kind of "monster hatch" effect that I've observed on a number of tailwaters. Most of these rivers have large populations of bugs, but as Professor Ward's work indicates, there are fewer *species* of bugs. What this means is that when hatches occur they can be pretty heavy and often include just one species.

In contrast, a free-flowing stream, or a tailwater quite a distance downstream from the dam, may have lighter hatches of a particular species but often has more multiple hatches where several species of insects are emerging at the same time. Small, sporadic hatches to which the trout may or may not respond can also occur.

What it all boils down to from a nympher's point of view is that on a typical tailwater there are periods of time, which can be lengthy, where absolutely nothing is happening on the water's surface. I've fished some tailwaters where the only bugs I've observed coming off the water for several days in a row were the occasional, very light midge hatches that were of interest only to juvenile trout.

It's also important to note, in fact *very* important to note, that a lack of surface activity doesn't mean the trout aren't feeding. Just put on your Polaroids and take a look down into the water. Pay special attention to where the water runs into pools and spreads out as it slows down. Look behind the rocks, study the tail sections of the pools, try to focus on the stream bottom below the less severe, nonpounding kind of riffles, check out the glides, watch any edge, seam, crease, or drop where water speed changes. Take a peek at every bit of bottom that you can, just in case.

If you are fishing a rich tailwater such as the Frying Pan or the South Platte or the Green you will probably have seen the outline of a trout in almost every one of those lies. You might even have caught a trout loafing around in some shallow, dead backwater where it shouldn't have been. What's more, you probably will have noted a quick flash or turn or maybe even caught a glimpse of the "big white" as a trout opened its mouth to feed on a nymph that had been caught up in the drift. If none of these trout are rising to the surface to take emerging or spent insects your mandate is clear—you will simply have to catch them where they are feeding.

WET FLIES

Fly fishermen have been trying to catch trout using imitations of the immature phases of aquatic insects for most of the sport's history. There's good reason to believe that wet flies were among the very first flies ever tied. By today's standards wet flies and wet-fly fishing techniques are thought of more as imitating emerging insects or acting simply as attractors rather than actually representing the bottom-dwelling, gilled nymphs associated with the nympher's art.

Although you will occasionally run into a real dyed-in-the-wool wet-fly fisherman, the simple truth is that the wet-fly fisherman's gentle art has for the most part been supplanted by nymphing techniques. I wouldn't totally count out the wet fly though, because it has a way of reviving itself as a popular fly fishing technique.

Wet-fly techniques were quite popular in the United States throughout the 1940s, 1950s, and even into the 1960s. It's still not hard to find the wet-fly action bamboo rods that were produced by the thousands during that period. These rods have the characteristic soft action that begins just above the handle of the rod. This type of action, which is a far cry from what today's anglers want, helped wet-fly fishermen with their down-and-across fly presentations and with the roll casts that were preferred for keeping the fly wet. The wet flies themselves were quite elegant and many of the patterns are considered classics.

There's a simple reason why the wet fly and wet-fly techniques never quite fade away. These techniques, along with an occasional variation, still catch trout. Although I do carry a few wet flies and have caught trout with them in many tailwaters, I'll be the first to admit that for catching trout below the water's surface I rely mainly on nymphing techniques.

NYMPHING HISTORY

Among those anglers who occasionally sit on a river's bank and talk about the progression of things, George Edward Mackenzie Skues, a London attorney, is generally considered as the first to organize nymphing techniques into any kind of system. His ideas appeared in several books from the early 1900s up until his opus, *Nymph Fishing for Chalk Stream Trout*, appeared in 1939. Skues is best remembered for the ongoing feud he engaged in with Frederick Halford, a strict dry-fly advocate, over the ethicality of nymph fishing.

While all of this was going on in England, legendary American fly fishermen such as Theodore Gordon, Edward Hewitt, and Preston Jennings, while mainly remembered for their contributions as dry-fly fishermen, were also experimenting with nymphing techniques. James Leisenring, a Pennsylvanian angler, actually corresponded with Skues and is only now receiving well-deserved recognition for his influence on American nymphing techniques.

Nymphing techniques in both tailwaters and free-flowing streams were dominated first by modified wet-fly techniques. As time progressed, fly tiers began adding weight to nymph imitations so that they would sink to the bottom. The introduction of sinking fly lines and Sink-Tip fly lines added a new dimension to nymphing in the 1960s.

DEAD DRIFT NYMPHING

The most influential innovation in nymph fishing as we know it today appears to have initially gained popularity on a number of Rocky Mountain tailwaters. The technique is most commonly known as *dead drift* or *short line nymphing* and is the dominant method used by anglers trying to catch trout that are feeding on or near the bottom. Actually, dead drift nymphing wasn't as much of an innovation in the way anglers thought about nymphing as it was a change in how they got the fly to the trout. The change revolved around where the weight was put to get the nymph imitation on the bottom.

Initially, anglers had noted that nymphs weighted under the dubbing with lead fuse wire wrapped around the hook shank were quite effective where the water wasn't too deep or too swift. The flies didn't cast worth a damn but by gosh they sure caught the trout. Later, the sinking lines and Sink-Tip lines gave nymphers a little more latitude, but they still had trouble getting nymphs down to trout in the deeper runs and in faster current. Finally, someone said the heck with it and clamped a split shot onto the leader about a foot above the nymph. By adding or taking off weight the angler could get the fly down to just about any trout in any lie on the river. This new rig didn't cast worth a damn either, but by this time nymphers had gotten used to the fact that casting nymphs just wasn't going to be as much fun as casting dry flies. The trade-off was that now and then you hooked into a hog trout—and it was more often *now* than then.

The basics of dead drift nymphing are pretty easy to understand. A nymph imitation is tied to the end of the tippet and about a foot to eighteen inches above that a weight is attached. Initially, many nymphers were partial to the kind of split shot that came with the little tabs that made them easy to remove from the leader. This type of weight made it

Dead drift nymphing techniques are an effective way to take tailwater trout that are feeding below the water's surface.

easy to quickly change the position or size of the weight on the leader.

The amount of weight added to the leader is very important because the idea in dead drifting is to get the nymph imitation down to where the trout are feeding, but once it's there you want it to drift along naturally with the current. Too much weight means the nymph won't drift at all, or if it does it won't appear natural. The price you pay for too much weight is that your split shot hangs up somewhere on the streambed and you end up breaking the fly off. Too little weight isn't quite so bad because all that happens is the imitation passes above the trout as it drifts downstream, but at least it doesn't get hung up. The problem is that you don't get many strikes, either!

If possible, I always try to locate trout visually when nymphing. It isn't that you can't catch fish in the deeper, hidden runs, but seeing trout puts the odds more in your favor. If I can see a trout feeding in a certain lie I always figure I have half the battle won. Besides, it's exciting. The other advantage is that there's no question when you've spooked the fish, so you don't have to waste time fishing empty water.

Once the trout is located and you attach the proper amount of weight to the leader (I almost always use unweighted nymph imitations), you need to get into position to cast to the trout. You'll be surprised how close you can get to actively nymphing trout, especially when you approach them from downstream where they are least likely to spot you. I don't know exactly why nymphing trout don't seem to spook as readily as surface feeders, but it's likely that they feel safer feeding in the deeper water. I've also wondered if they might just get used to fishermen because tailwaters tend to get so much fishing pressure. All I know is that the trout in my favorite smaller streams and many larger free-flowing streams I've fished tend to be a lot spookier when nymphing than their counterparts in tailwaters.

Anyway, it pays to get as close to the nymphing trout as possible. Once you're in position, make a quick mental calculation of how far upstream above the trout you will have to cast for the nymph imitation to settle to the bottom and begin drifting naturally to the trout. This depends on both the velocity and depth of the water. The faster the water is moving, the farther upstream you'll need to cast the rig. The same is true for depth—the deeper the water the farther upstream the cast.

I've found that in all but a few special cases nymphing trout move very little to take a fly. Expect the trout to station themselves in a feeding lane and remain right there, letting the current bring the nymphs to them. That means casts have to be right on the money—your nymph imitation has to drift right in front of the feeding trout! Your saving grace here is that if you do miscalculate a drift you'll seldom spook the trout. Just pick up the fly after it drifts past the feeding trout and make another, hopefully more accurate, cast.

There is a basic geometric formula you can use to calculate the way your fly rod should be positioned as the nymph imitation bounces along the stream bottom toward the trout. Try to hold the rod as close to parallel to the water's surface as possible. This will help keep the leader perpendicular to the water's surface when the fly is in the strike zone, that is, where the trout are. To achieve this you'll have to be fairly close to the trout and you should follow the nymph imitation with the rod tip as it moves downstream. Following the nymph with the rod tip will keep slack out of the line, maintain the necessary right angle between the leader and water, and extend the natural-looking dead drift before line drag develops.

Fly Fishing the Tailwaters

The point to all the geometry is that it helps you detect strikes. You'll need to rivet your attention on the leader where it enters the water. If it hesitates in the least, moves slightly upstream, stops dead, starts out slowly across the current, or acts unusual in any way, set the hook. In the beginning expect to catch anything *but* trout—the bottom, sticks, vegetation, and other anglers if they are fishing to close to you. But you'll get the hang of it after a while.

Nymphing trout are notorious for "soft-taking" imitations. Strikes are just plain hard to detect for anglers who are new to the game. At least in the beginning, it isn't uncommon to get a strike and never know it! With practice you might "see" the strike but respond after the trout has already rejected the fly. This can result in a foul-hooked trout, the polite way of saying the trout has been hooked in a part of its body other than the mouth.

Becoming a good nympher requires a certain degree of stubbornness. You just have to stick with it until you've caught a few trout, preferably in the mouth. It doesn't take many trout before you begin to get a feel for what constitutes a strike as opposed to your fly nicking the bottom or momentarily catching a strand of vegetation. As you become more and more experienced in the nympher's art you find that your reflexes become so finely tuned that you won't even know why you set the hook when you did—you'll only know that you've gotten another trout on! It ultimately works down to the most subtle, almost subliminal signals that tell you a trout has taken your offering.

That's basically the way I learned to nymph about twenty years ago on the South Platte River. While the basics of reading the water and detecting strikes are still the same, a lot of technology has developed around the nympher's art.

STRIKE INDICATORS

Strike indicators came right on the heels of the dead drift nymphing revolution. A strike indicator was exactly what it said—it helped you "see" strikes more clearly. Anglers were quick to realize that, while they could catch nymphing trout by concentrating carefully on where the leader entered the water, it was a lot easier to detect strikes if, say, an inch-long piece of brightly colored fly line was threaded onto their leader. It was much easier to focus attention on the brightly colored strike indicator as it moved downstream rather than the transparent leader. Even the most delicate takes by wary trout became detectable. An added advantage was that the strike indicators made absolute line control less critical. A little slack line on the water wouldn't result in quite so many flubbed strikes because the strike indicator, not the entry point of the leader into the water, was now the focus of the nympher's attention. This also meant that longer casts could be undertaken as long as the strike indicator was visible and reasonable care was taken with line mending chores and the management of excessive slack. It also made nymphing on windy days, when the water's surface was ruffled up, considerably easier.

There has been a proliferation of strike indicators that use a snippet of brightly colored material attached to the leader. You can purchase stick-on fluorescent tabs; fly lines with brightly colored tips that serve as strike indicators; and brightly dyed, knotless, tapered leaders. Or you can just tie a brightly colored piece of yarn onto your leader at the appropriate place. Any of these products can help in the detection of strikes. Which one, if any, you use is a matter of personal choice.

There is one other kind of strike indicator that is very popular. This variety actually started out as a small cork that was painted in a Day-Glo color and attached to the leader. Although the original cork strike indicators are still available, there are also a number of more high-tech polystyrene renditions. These are the type of indicators that fishing guides will often put on a beginning sport's line to help him detect strikes. These indicators essentially act like a bobber and are quite effective in helping an angler see strikes.

The bobber-like indicators also make long-line nymphing more effective. An angler can cast this rig quite a distance and still see the indicator well enough to detect strikes. Another advantage is that the bobber-like indicator does have a degree of buoyancy and can be adjusted on the leader to a level that is roughly the depth of the water that the angler intends to nymph. This extra little bit of flotation can help dead drift the imitation in a very natural fashion. This float can also make it possible to nymph edges, creases, and seams in rough water conditions where it is impossible to see any other kind of strike indicator.

Fly Fishing the Tailwaters

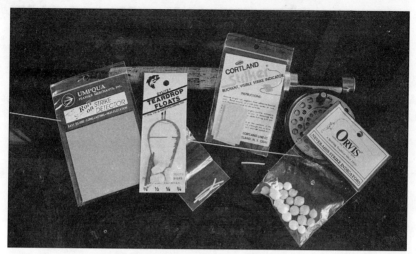

Strike indicators come in a variety of sizes and shapes.

I know of one stretch on the Frying Pan River where in the springtime when the water was high there was a particularly productive crease between two tongues of rough water. It was one of those situations where you needed your wading staff to get into position. I remember fishing there for the better part of a morning without getting a single strike, although I occasionally glimpsed the movements of trout under the water's surface. I finally came to the conclusion that if I was getting strikes at all, I was missing them because my strike indicator was often lost to view in the rough water.

I switched to a bobber-like indicator, adjusted it for depth carefully, and ended up catching trout for the rest of the afternoon. A number of them went over 20 inches! It turned out that this crease was a bit of an untapped resource in spite of receiving plenty of fishing pressure. Although many anglers were drifting nymphs along the quick-moving edges of the crease, they either had their weight calculated wrong, which would mean their offerings weren't getting down to the trout, or they just weren't seeing the strikes.

One final point about strike indicators. If you choose to use one, figure that sooner or later someone will tell you in so many words that you might as well be a bait fisherman, what with the bobber and all. The point here is that the purity issue that was a part of the little tiff between

The lead weight used by dead drift nymphers to get their flies down deep comes in many sizes and styles.

Halford and Skues is still in the air—and it often comes out in relation to strike indicators. It has died down a bit over the past few years as more and more fly fishermen are drawn to nymphing.

I think I've just about run the gamut of nymphing techniques and gizmos. I started off with no strike indicator at all, then worked into the brightly colored little piece of fly line on the leader. I eventually set up a complete nymphing rig on another spool that I used when it came time to nymph. I even experimented with flat monofilament line in place of a fly line for nymphing very deep holes. As it stands now, I've come full circle back to no strike indicator. There is no philosophical basis to it at all—I just got tired of changing spools and diddling around when I wanted to do some dead drift nymphing, so I opted for simplicity even though I sometimes catch a few less trout. I still carry strike indicators for unusual situations and would recommend them if you're just learning how to dead drift a nymph. They'll make your life a whole lot easier.

The other big difference between dead drifting then and now has to do with the weights available to put on the leader. When I started out on the South Platte you were basically limited to split shot or lead strips known as Twist-ons. Some enterprising nymphers used fuse wire. Today there are a variety of possibilities. I'm looking at a fly fishing catalog right now

Fly Fishing the Tailwaters

that devotes an entire page to lead weights and strike indicators. You can get Nymph Strips, Soft Lead, split shot in any size, or a lead or copper sleeve that slips over the leader. The thing to consider when you're looking at the various possibilities is which particular kind of weight will snag the least. It's sort of subjective because I'll guarantee they'll all snag sooner or later and you *will* lose flies and tippet material. Pick the lead that makes you feel the best.

FINE TUNING THE DEAD DRIFT

Okay, once you've got all your dead drift nymphing doodads together and you've made your first couple of attempts at nymphing and probably have lost two or three dozen flies and a pound of lead, you're ready to catch your first trout. The odds are this fish will hook itself, but you'll learn something. The next trout you catch will teach you more, particularly about the mysteries of detecting strikes. It can be mysterious, too. You will get to where you hook trout and aren't even aware of going through any kind of process. My theory is that, with time, this strike detecting business gets internalized to the point that it resides solely in the autonomic nervous system. All I'm saying is that if you find yourself going through a "mystical" period in your nymphing, don't worry. It happens to all of us.

There are some ways to fine tune your dead drift nymphing skills once you've learned the basics. The first is to consider where you are placing the weight on the leader and how that affects the fly's behavior. Weight placed closer to the fly will keep it closer to the bottom. Using a nymph imitation that has been weighted and attaching weight to the leader about six inches above it will allow you to literally crawl that imitation along the stream bottom.

Conversely, putting the weight farther up the leader allows the imitation more freedom of movement. Remember this, especially when you see the trout becoming more active underwater. If they are slashing about and leaving their feeding lanes the odds are that the beginning phase of a hatch is on and the trout are picking off the first of the emerging insects. This is the time to move the location of the weight up the leader, maybe as far as twenty to twenty-five inches, and use an unweighted imitation. You may also want to switch to the lightest tippet possible: 5X is generally the lightest you can get away with, although 6X is possible in the most delicate situations where the water is fairly placid.

The lighter tippets allow the currents in the water to impart more action to the nymph, which adds to the effect you'll gain when the unweighted fly wells up along the current edges. This makes the imitation appear very much like an emerging bug to the increasingly frenzied trout. It can be a deadly technique.

Another trick to try before the dry-fly stages of a hatch is to allow the nymph imitation to swing with the current at the end of each drift. This, of course, can't be considered a dead drift; nonetheless, it is often effective. The fly naturally begins to rise at the end of a drift, which makes for another good way to simulate the emerging bugs. Actually, letting the fly swing to the surface at the end of each drift is worthwhile whether a hatch is imminent or not because the quick movement of the fly toward the surface will sometimes coax the trout into a strike.

Another possibility is to employ a dropper. This simply means that you fish two nymphs instead of one. There are a number of strategies for determining which flies to use. Some nymphers swear by an emerger tied to the end of the tippet and a nymph on a dropper above it. The weight is then attached to the leader about a foot above the dropper. Other people have other theories. I usually just use two different flies, either of which I think has a chance to score. It's that simple.

Depending on who you talk to, how you attach the dropper can turn into a nightmare of mind-boggling complexities. The best and simplest system I've found is to attach the weight to the leader at a knot and about eight or ten inches down from that tie in the first fly with an improved clinch knot, trimming off the excess tippet material when the knot is completed. Now, through the hook eye of the nymph you just tied on, tie in another length of tippet material with an improved clinch knot. This piece of tippet can be anywhere from a foot to twenty inches in length. Tie your other imitation to the end of this length of tippet, again with an improved clinch knot.

This system (it's actually a non-dropper, two fly system) not only works as well as other more complex systems, but it also is less prone to the tan-

Fly Fishing the Tailwaters

The Gold-Ribbed Hare's Ear, an excellent general purpose tailwater nymph imitation, tied on a dropper.

gles inherent in many dropper systems. One word of caution: If you are like me and in the habit of running your hand down from the weight along the tippet to find your fly, this dropper system will cure you of it fast. It only takes getting hooked by the first fly a few times.

While developing a real facility with dropper systems probably isn't critical to your future as a tailwater nympher, it does give you a little more latitude for fishing the nymph imitations and can be a *real* scream if you luck into a double.

Roy Palm, the dean of an entire school of excellent fly fishermen who live and guide in the vicinity of the Frying Pan River, showed me a useful refinement that has improved my nymphing technique. He suggested that rather than holding the fly rod exactly parallel to the river as I followed the nymph on its drift downstream, I should consider angling the tip up about 20 to 30 degrees. This angle gives you more control over any slack line that might accumulate on the water and allows you to see strikes more clearly. I'm a convert.

On occasion you will find that your nymphing goals will be best served by removing the weight from the leader. Sometimes a nymph tied with a touch of weight under the dubbing and cast upstream into shallow riffles will be tremendously productive. You need to be a good line manager to pull this off, though, since any excessive slack that accumulates on the water will lessen your chances of hooking the trout. This same weighted-nymph technique is also a lot of fun when working shallow pocket water. I just wade slowly upstream popping the fly into every pocket that shows promise.

You might also want to learn the hand-twist retrieve for working slow backwaters and sloughs. The fly line is retrieved with a folding motion where your hand is placed under the line, little finger toward the reel, with the line hooked loosely around the index finger. The line can then be retrieved by looping it over the little finger while pulling the loop off the index finger with the middle fingers of the line hand. The loop is then pulled off the little finger and gathered into the palm of the hand. The process is repeated until all the line has been retrieved. Although it sounds difficult, a fly fisherman who has experience with the hand-twist retrieve can teach it to you in a few minutes.

The basics of short-line dead drift nymphing: The nymph imitation with weight attached to the leader is cast upstream from nymphing trout. The rod is angled up about 30 degrees to help with line management.

A weighted nymph cast to trout cruising a backwater and then hand-twisted back can be deadly. Also, the hand-twist retrieve can be utilized at the end of a standard drift when dead drift nymphing. Instead of lifting the imitation out of the water and casting again, hand twist it back upstream. This goes against the rules, but you'd be surprised.

IMITATIONS

When it comes to the exact imitation you will be putting on the end of the tippet, I believe you can cover more ground if your nymph imitations are impressionistic. If you enjoy tying really precise renditions of various species of nymphs, this doesn't mean you should stop. The entomological research you'll need to do for that kind of precision tying will probably improve your knowledge of stream ecology and make you a better angler in the process. All I'm saying is that I don't believe the trout will hold it against you if your *Tricorythodes* imitation has two tails instead of three.

My major concerns for tailwater nymph imitations are pretty basic—I look at *size*, *color*, *action*, and *outline*. The size of the imitation you use

An angler watches the strike indicator or the leader where it enters the water. As the nymph imitation drifts through the strike zone, the angler watches for any hesitation, unnatural motion, or abrupt stops that could indicate the fly has been taken.

The angler continues to observe the strike indicator at the end of the drift. Sometimes a fly that is lifted slowly or allowed to swing at the end of the drift will induce a strike.

will be determined by inspection or intuition. On most tailwaters within four or so miles of the dam, it's safe to assume that if the trout aren't working the midges they're probably taking mayfly or caddisfly nymphs in the #18 to #14 hook-size range. You'll find variations, of course, but they'll almost always be special situations, like the Green Drake hatch on the Frying Pan River where the nymphs are huge and you can't miss them. If you're in doubt, kick over a few rocks and seine the drift to determine the size of the fly you need.

I try to have a range of colors but I concentrate on tans, browns, blacks, and particularly olives. I've found that olive-colored nymphs are effective on many tailwaters. This may be because it's common for tailwaters to have a greenish or olive-colored streambed due to the algae and aquatic vegetation that grow there. I've found that nymphs often assume colors that are close to those of the streambed where they live. The Frying Pan River is a case in point. The streambed there is characterized by reddish-pink rocks. A Pale Morning Dun nymph that tends to be a brown to a brown-olive color in other tailwaters will be a lighter brown tinged with pink on the Frying Pan.

I think the action of a nymph is the most important aspect of the fly.

Under this heading I include the ability of the imitation to capture air bubbles, which add to its flash and make it appear more natural to the trout. I tie most of my nymphs with dyed, picked-out rabbit fur because I think it helps to trap the air and has a breathing, lifelike quality in the water. I'm also a big fan of marabou and other down feather materials that are included in nymph patterns. I'm not sure whether these materials imitate gills or simply trap air, but the action they impart to the fly certainly seems attractive to trout. The latest craze is the flashback nymph imitation where a flashy synthetic material like Flashabou is tied into the fly as a wing case. This gives the fly an added flash of the same variety that air trapped into the body dubbing gives.

The outline the nymph presents is important, too. There are two varieties. The first I described above as having a flashy, trapped-air, picked-out look. You'll see this type of look in many Gold-Ribbed Hare's Ear type patterns. The other outline is the opposite and has a sleeker, more traditional look. It has thin tails and abdomen along with a fatter thorax section and wing case. I use it most often in Pheasant Tail nymph patterns, which work very well for imitating the *Baetis* species that are often a major component in tailwater fisheries. The classic March Brown nymph pattern also presents this type of outline.

There are some specialized flies, although not technically nymphs, that you'll want to have in your fly box when you hit the tailwaters. Scud or freshwater shrimp patterns in sizes #18 through #12 are important. I carry them in orange, pink, olive, and gray. Scuds are often very important trout foods in close proximity to bottom-release dams. Their importance may diminish as you move farther downstream. On some tailwaters scud imitations are a factor year-round, while on others you may find them most important during high water in the spring. These imitations are most effectively fished using dead drift nymphing techniques.

Aquatic worm imitations, also known as San Juan worms, are another must for your tailwater fly box. These patterns come in a variety of designs. My preference is for the very simply tied patterns where a strand of Ultra Chenille is lashed down to the hook shank. For a while, English bait hooks were popular for tying worm imitations. Although this hook made a good-looking fly, I now avoid it because of the inherent poor-hooking qualities of the design. I've also seen cases where it

Scuds are important trout food in many tailwaters. These imitations are best fished using dead drift nymphing techniques.

causes damage to the trout's eye by hooking up through the roof of the trout's mouth and out through the eye.

You should have San Juan worms in a variety of colors, paying particular attention to reds, oranges, yellows, tans, and browns. These aquatic worms are often quite ubiquitous in tailwaters. It's a good imitation to use if nothing particular is happening and you're trying to drum up a few strikes. Dead drift this fly right on the bottom.

As discussed in chapter 2, you'd best not leave home without at least a few of the giant stonefly imitations. I don't usually carry many unless I'm going to a tailwater where I know populations of these big guys occur. If that is the case, I pack plenty of them.

Finally, I like to include a few leech patterns and Woolly Buggers as attractor patterns for dead drifting. Both patterns can be fished quite effectively using dead drift techniques. I usually weight my Woolly Buggers but not my leech patterns. You'd be amazed at the number of trout you can pick up on a dead afternoon by just drifting a Woolly Bugger or leech through the deeper runs and riffles. The Buggers are also effective when fished using standard streamer techniques.

A final point to remember about patterns is that whenever you're fishing a tailwater that's new to you, touch base with the locals to make sure there isn't some special phenomenon that you need to know about. Something off the wall like a cranefly pattern may be particularly important and you'll want to buy a few of them at the local fly shop.

STREAMER FISHING

The final underwater diversion that you may want to consider for tailwater trout is the streamer. I'll admit that I'm probably not the person to talk to about streamer fishing the tailwaters because I tend to get so wrapped up in the nymphing that I only get around to tying on a streamer as a last resort. This is despite the fact that some tailwaters do seem to have reasonable populations of baitfish. In fact, I know some anglers who specialize in fishing streamers in tailwaters, particularly where big brown trout are to be found.

My one big streamer experience on a tailwater was what I call my "Zonker" summer on the South Platte. The Zonker summer occurred when my friend Dana Tellin, who lives on the Arkansas River, turned me on to Zonkers. These are Matuka-style streamers tied with a fixed rabbit-fur wing and mylar body rather than a feather wing and dubbed body. These streamers have incredible action and are deadly. Anyway, I had so much fun catching trout on the Arkansas with them that I vowed to spend a whole summer fishing them in the Cheeseman Canyon catch-and-release section of the South Platte, where trout are often extremely selective to very small flies. I reasoned that it would be a good way to learn how to fish streamers.

By using traditional streamer techniques where I cast the fly across the river and then let it swing downstream, I kept busy catching trout. I also used a trick Dana had taught me where you cast the weighted Zonker upstream and retrieve it back as fast as possible. These techniques caught trout, especially early and late in the day, and even once in a while during the midday lulls that often occur on a trout stream. I didn't catch nearly as many trout as I would have caught nymphing, but it was an education just to know these selective fish were vulnerable to streamer tactics.

It was also kind of fun to land trout near another angler who was patiently nymphing a #22 midge pupa imitation. When he'd yell downstream, "What are you using?" and I'd answer back, "A number four Zonker," his jaw would drop into the river.

Since the Zonker summer I've used streamers now and then when the water levels change, when the water is discolored, or when the fishing is just generally off. Zonkers, Spruce Flies, and Muddler Minnows are my favorites.

You should be aware of one streamer situation in tailwaters that occurs in the stilling basin directly below the dam. This can be prime water for streamer techniques. I'm fond of crawling a Woolly Bugger, with a split shot fastened to the leader right at the eye of the hook, very slowly along the bottom of the stilling basin. Another option is to use a Sink-Tip line. A Sink-Tip line with a two-foot-long leader and a Woolly Bugger or leech attached can make for some fun there. If you haven't gotten enough fishing after an entire day on the river, remember that some of the very best stilling-basin streamer fishing occurs after dark.

READING THE WATER

Sooner or later you will find yourself in the situation where you won't be able to sight-fish to nymphing trout. It could be that the particular tailwater you're working has a number of deep runs, or maybe a water release has made the river murky. Whatever the reason, you will have to learn to read the water. What this means in a nutshell is that you'll be fishing where you *think* the trout should be.

The ability to figure out where trout should be is curious. Some anglers just naturally seem to "know," while others never quite get the hang of it. Entire books have been written on reading water that detail and rate just about every place in the river that a trout might choose to lie. The trout's locations depend on a number of factors such as whether they're feeding or hiding or simply stacked up because of the natural pecking order in their particular pool or riffle. When nymphing you should concentrate on trying to find feeding trout.

My main strategy is to find edges. Edges in a river are created in two basic ways: by two or more columns of water that are moving at different speeds coming together, or by the actual structure of the streambed itself. These edges not only act as traps where trout food caught in the drift will "fall out" but they also afford good holding areas for trout. Once you get this edge concept in your mind you'll begin to see trout holding and feeding lies all over the river. You'll see an edge where a fast column of water tumbles into the still water of a pool. You'll see the microedges created by the rubble on the bottom of a riffle. You'll look for trout where the streambed shelves off.

A point to remember if you're nymphing to trout you can't see is to try to mark very clearly in your mind exactly where it is that you get your strikes. The interplay of currents can be quite complex in, say, the deeper runs, and the trout will often be congregated in a tight pod in a very precise location. Odds are they won't move an inch one way or another to take your imitation. If, after you've caught your first trout from the run, you've marked the drift that your nymph made on that cast and can duplicate it, you may very well pull four or five or more trout out of that exact same lie!

Like any kind of "reading," the best way to get good at reading water is to practice. When you're on the river don't just nymph a certain kind of water where you know you'll catch trout. Make hypotheses about different types of edges, then test them. You'd be surprised at the places you'll find trout where you had only an inkling they'd be.

The most interesting water-reading situation I ever encountered occurred on the San Juan River in northern New Mexico. There is a long, almost perfectly flat, glassy glide there that's about four to five feet deep. It's the kind of water that makes you feel illiterate because there appears to be nothing to read—it's just a big, featureless mass of water moving downstream at the same speed.

I chose to fish it in that time-honored salmon fisherman's tradition. I took three steps downstream and nymphed the water starting in close and working my way out. If I didn't get a strike after covering the water thoroughly I took three more steps downstream and repeated the procedure.

I finally hooked into a nice rainbow trout using these searching tactics but by then I'd developed a hypothesis. As I'd been moving downstream I'd occasionally felt small depressions in the silt that had collected on the stream bottom of the glide. The depressions came in groups and that's where I caught the trout. It occurred to me that these very shallow depressions might create just enough of an "edge" that the trout would hold in them. I continued searching the streambed with my feet

The stilling basins located directly beneath many dams can be successfully fished by crawling a weighted Woolly Bugger across the bottom.

for the depressions and in the process landed a couple of good trout. You'd have never guessed they'd have been there, either!

Nowadays, the options available in both equipment and techniques is amazing for those fly fishermen who want to catch trout from below the water's surface. In fact, it seems like the real thrust in fly fishing the tailwaters over the past decade or so has been in the realm of fishing nymphs. Longer, faster action graphite rods coupled with improved techniques have really made catching deep-water, nymphing trout much more of a possibility than it used to be.

With practice, concentration, and a good sense of humor, nymphing for tailwater trout could very well become an important component of your days astream, too.

CHAPTER 5

When the Trout Rise–
Dry Flies, Emergers, and Some Razzle-Dazzle

T AILWATER TROUT HAVE a solid reputation for selectivity when rising to the classic dry-fly hatches. If you are ever in the mood to hear some stories of despair, just show up at the Icebox Pool on the South Platte River after the Blue-Winged Olive hatch. That's a place where the entire lower end of the pool may be covered, bank to bank, with rising trout for the duration of a three-hour-long hatch. It's also a place where highly skilled dry-fly fishermen are happy to have landed two or three trout *between* them over that three-hour period.

Tailwater risers tend to be selective feeders more often than their cousins that inhabit unregulated rivers. Trout become selective for many reasons and a number of these are evident in tailwaters. Generally there's more fishing pressure, which makes trout warier, if not wiser; the water is clearer, making trout spookier and pickier; and there are fewer species of insects in the trout's diet so that they key more precisely on the bugs that are available.

These factors occur in addition to the universals like weather and air temperature, which affect the fishing whether you're on a tailwater or not. The point here is that you will have to go to the tailwaters *prepared* for selectively rising trout. That's just playing the percentages, but you don't have to turn this selectivity business into a religion. If you fish the tailwaters enough, sooner or later you'll be on the river when the much written about, harder than hell to catch, "selective" trout are as playful as cutthroats that have never been fished over. Think of selectivity as a function of conditions. Keep in mind that these are trout, not bodhisattvas.

MAYFLIES AND TAILWATERS

Okay, now that I've got that off my chest we can get down to business. There are a few generalities that can be made, particularly about mayfly species inhabiting tailwaters. Of course, these generalities come with all the standard disclaimers. When fishing the hatches on the tailwaters it always pays to keep an open mind to exceptions and to new ways of looking at old problems.

With that said, here are a few things to remember. Figure as a rule of thumb that the closer you are to the dam the greater the likelihood that you will encounter the smaller-size mayfly species. Expect to encounter larger-size species as you move downstream from the dam.

When you are fishing tailwaters that occur below a bottom-release dam where very cold water is released, you might also encounter a "dead spot" in relation to hatches and trout activity right below the dam and for a short distance downstream. This effect, when it does occur, is most likely because of the very cold water suppressing insect life.

The length of the dead spot varies with each tailwater. But as the water warms into the 40-degree (Fahrenheit) range you'll begin to find better hatches and, most importantly, more trout activity. As you move downstream these single-species hatches will increase in magnitude. You'll also begin to encounter a few additional mayfly species. Finally, the point will come when the sheer numbers of mayflies produced in a hatch by any one species will decrease. The complexity of hatches involving multiple species will increase but fewer bugs will be produced overall. At this point, the river's insect populations will increasingly resemble an unregulated river.

When considering mayflies as trout food, fly fishermen must be concerned with four life stages of the insect. The nymph is the immature phase of the mayfly that lives underwater; the emergent phase covers the short period of time when the nymph, which has reached its final phase of development, moves toward the water's surface, where the nymphal shuck splits and the initial winged adult form emerges.

Fly fishermen refer to this recently hatched mayfly adult as the *dun* or, more scientifically, the *subimago*. The dun is best characterized by its relatively opaque wings. The dun then goes through a final molt, changing into the *spinner* or *imago*. The time it takes for this transformation to occur depends on the species, but for most it occurs within a day. The imago is characterized by transparent wings and a shiny body. In some cases the dun and spinner of the same species may have very different coloration.

The sole biological purpose of the spinner phase is for reproduction. This occurs when females fly into swarms of males in order to be fertilized. These breeding swarms often occur quickly after the final molt. Once the females deposit their fertilized eggs into the water, they die and fall spent with their wings flat out on the water's surface where they are often taken by the trout. Dry-fly fishermen are concerned with mayflies as emergers, as duns and spinners, and as spent spinners, since the trout are feeding on or near the surface during all of these phases.

BLUE-WINGED OLIVES

There are several groups of mayflies that seem to occur in tailwaters with regularity. Among these, the Blue-Winged Olives may very well be the most ubiquitous. Actually, what fly fishermen across the nation refer to in general as the "Blue-Winged Olives" aren't really any single species of mayfly. The fact is that the Blue-Winged Olive may represent as many as fifteen or twenty different species of mayflies.

If you are a "match the hatch" sort of fly fisherman let me make something clear before panic sets in. It will not be necessary to have an imitation of every one of these species. All of them are characterized during the hatch by grayish blue wings and bodies that range from a light olive yellow to an almost brown or reddish olive. The operative word here is *olive*. The other characteristic these mayflies have in common is that they tend to be small, ranging in size anywhere from 4 to 7 millimeters in length. This translates to about a #22 to #16 standard dry-fly hook.

For those who would like to get into a little more detail, I would suggest studying two specific genera of mayflies that fall into the Blue-Winged Olive realm. These genera, *Baetis* and *Pseudocloeon*, seem to be considered the most important by experts who know more than I do. The *Baetis* species are more commonly the larger Blue-Winged Olives that you see in the 6-millimeter to 7-millimeter sizes, whereas the *Pseudocloeon* are the tiny 4-millimeter to 5-millimeter Blue-Winged Olives that will get you into the #22 hook size range.

Hatches of Blue-Winged Olives are best known among anglers for the time of the season when they occur. Most fly fishermen associate these bugs with the first dependable mayfly hatch of the season and the last dependable hatch of the year. The Blue-Winged Olives are also often associated with overcast, rainy, or just generally nasty conditions. On tailwaters, Blue-Winged Olives of one species or another are usually hatching from the earliest stormy days of springtime until the beginning months of the summer. They come on strongly again in the late autumn or even occasionally on a winter afternoon.

The reason you don't hear so much about them during the milder months is that they are a smaller mayfly whose importance is often overshadowed by more spectacular hatches of larger species of mayflies later in the season. The important point to remember about tailwater Blue-Winged Olives is that they can be tremendously abundant, especially early and late in the season.

This is doubly true the closer you get to the dam, where the likelihood of encountering hatches of the larger species of mayflies is diminished. I concentrate my dry-fly efforts on the emergent and dun phases of the Blue-Winged Olives. Although you will sometimes come across excellent spinner falls, they often occur only in the morning before many anglers have made their way to the river. When the spinner fall does occur later in the day, watch out—it may provide the best fishing you see all day.

TRICOS

Another mayfly that many tailwater fly fishermen, both East and West, have become accustomed to is the Tiny White-Winged Black. The

Dry flies and emergers come in an array of different styles. Pictured here from the traditionally tied dry fly at the top are (clockwise): a no-hackle Compara-dun, a parachute hackled paradun, a parachute hackled floating nymph, two different emerger patterns that show wings in different stages of development, and two more paradun dry flies.

chances of finding this little mayfly increases in tailwaters where slow, well-vegetated stretches of water are found. This is prime Tiny White-Winged Black habitat. These flies account for several species in the genus *Tricorythodes* and are, as the name implies, quite small, ranging from 3 to 7 millimeters. I never use much larger than a #18 standard dry-fly hook to imitate one. More average hook sizes are in the #20 to #22 range. The flies have white wings that are fairly broad for their size and the males in particular have dark, almost black, bodies. In some parts of the country the females may have a more olive hue.

It's safe to say that among the mayflies, the Tricos, as many tail-water anglers refer to them, provide the most exasperating dry-fly fishing. These mayflies follow a somewhat unusual cycle in that they hatch in the early morning and both male and female duns molt almost immediately into the spinner phase. Breeding occurs soon thereafter and on many rivers both the males and females have fallen

A paradun dry fly (left) compared with a traditionally tied dry fly (right). The paradun is the more effective dry fly for selective tailwater trout.

Pictured here are paradun (left) and hackled floating nymph (right). Rising trout that refuse the paradun will often take the floating nymph.

spent to the water's surface by ten or eleven in the morning!

Although it's quite possible to fish this hatch during the emergent and dun phases, the spinner fall is by far the point most anglers choose to enter the fray. For the uninitiated angler, the small-size spinner imitations are sometimes the focus of frustration. Amazingly enough, it is often possible to bump imitations up a hook size or two and still get strikes.

The real exasperation with the Tricos stems from contending with the fantastic numbers of them that often fall to the water. I've seen spent Tricos literally cover the water's surface in the calmer, slower sections

Fly Fishing the Tailwaters

of the river where they tend to hatch! Along with this abundance goes a certain kind of selectivity among the trout. The trout will seldom move out of their feeding lanes at all as the slow currents bring the spent Tricos right to them where they can be casually sipped.

Consequently, casts have to be made quite accurately to the feeding trout. Even perfect presentations are often refused. The game with the Tricos is perseverance. A particular trout may require ten or twenty presentations before it takes an artificial imitation. Once the trout is "on," the smaller flies and lighter tippets require a bit of a delicate touch to bring the fish to net.

The importance of the Trico hatch on the tailwaters where it occurs shouldn't be underestimated. For the angler willing to be on the water early it can be a mainstay of superlative dry-fly fishing from the early summer months into September. In many cases it is the Tricos that fill in the gap between the classic, large-size mayfly hatches of the early summer and the late-season fall hatches.

THE LARGER MAYFLIES

Any real continuity between eastern and western tailwaters breaks down when you begin to talk about the large-size mayflies that most of us consider as comprising the "classic" hatches. Many tailwaters, particularly as you get closer to the dams, seem to have limited populations of mayflies much bigger than 8 to 9 millimeters. Exceptions, of course, do occur. In the West you must consider the Green Drakes, which are a tremendous factor in some tailwaters but are absent or occur in inconsequential populations in others. Eastern and midwestern tailwaters, particularly as you move north, offer a smorgasbord of possibilities with the potential for hatches of March Browns, eastern Green Drakes, and Brown Drakes. Although a hatch of the big mayflies is always possible, it is still the smaller species that will be your bread and butter as a tailwater fly fisherman. Since it seems that the larger mayfly species are often affected by specific local conditions, their occurrence in a particular tailwater, either East or West, is best ascertained by local inquiry.

A final, though even more fragile, generalization about eastern and western tailwaters that I've found to be true is that pale-colored mayflies of several species appear well suited to conditions below dams. In the West, the Pale Morning Dun is probably the most important of the mayflies in the 6 millimeter to 9 millimeter range. In fact, a western tail-water angler supplied with Blue-Winged Olive, Trico, and Pale Morning Dun imitations is probably equipped to handle the major mayfly hatches he'll meet. In the East, the Sulphurs provide a rough equivalent to the Pale Morning Dun although they are not quite so widespread.

MAYFLY PATTERN STRATEGY

You can probably see that I'm beginning to pussyfoot around this mayfly thing a little and you're right. It doesn't take long for the gener-alizations to run out and for much of the information to get "stream spe-cific." That means you have to figure things out for yourself on the spe-cific tailwater you're fishing. Mayfly lore is sacred territory among fly fishers and you *will* find exceptions to all the rules, especially as you become more familiar with a particular tailwater.

There are some things you can do in a general way to increase the odds that you'll have imitations in your fly box that might just fool some trout in the mayfly situations you're *most* likely to encounter while fly fishing the tailwaters. My general plan for mayfly hatches on the tailwaters includes flies tied to imitate the emergent, dun, and spent spinner phases. I tie these patterns with the bodies dubbed in five key colors: brown, tan, olive, pale yellow, and black (or very dark brown). I use dyed rabbit as a base for all my body dubbing and use a little blend-ing trick to extend the range of each color a bit. Rather than dub bodies from "straight" colors, I make a loose blend, say, of olive with a little pale yellow, or pale yellow with a bit of bright neon-yellow acrylic material. Then, when I actually dub the fly bodies, I pull different shades of color from the loose blend. I don't know if it really makes that much difference, but I like to think that I'll have a little more latitude if the trout turn out to be persnickety.

I was tying some flies along the lines of this formula one evening when my friend John Gierach stopped by and reiterated a golden rule of

Fly Fishing the Tailwaters

The dry-fly box of an effective tailwater angler includes paradun dry flies with both quill and dubbed bodies along with emerger and floating nymph patterns.

the experimental fly tier that also applies to those of us who mess with differently shaded fur blends.

"Whatever you do, always tie at least two, and preferably three or four, of whatever it is you're tying. If you don't you can be damned sure that sooner or later the trout will want that one fly in your box that has no duplicate," John said.

He's right about it, too, except he forgot to mention that if you do end up in the "one fly situation" you'll probably break that one fly off on your third or fourth trout at the beginning of a three-hour-long hatch!

Anyway, I end up with an array of flies that are basically dubbed tan, brown, pale yellow, olive, and black. In terms of hook sizes, I concentrate my efforts on #20s through #14s. This doesn't mean you won't run into a big bruising Green Drake hatch or some other B-52 flying over the river. But if something like that does come off, its reputation almost always precedes it. In that case, you'll know in advance and can spend the night before your fishing trip furiously tying imitations.

Picking the style of fly you want to use to imitate the various phases of the mayfly can get pretty complicated these days. The proliferation of patterns over the past couple of decades has been phenomenal and the simple fact is that many of them work very well. After a number of years of experimenting with various dun patterns I've become a believer in patterns tied with a parachute hackle for my general purpose mayfly patterns. Swisher and Richards aptly called them *paraduns* in *Selective Trout*. These flies utilize a hackle that is wound horizontally around a post of wing material that allows the body of the fly to rest directly on the water's surface.

Not only does the paradun present a more realistic silhouette to the trout, but once you get the hang of it, it's easier to tie than the standard dry-fly patterns. I think some misconceptions evolved around the paradun patterns when a revival of their usage was aroused in the early 1970s. A number of patterns were evolved to fool very selective trout feeding in flat, calm water. These paraduns utilized the barest wisp of hackle—maybe just a couple of turns—to float them. It seems the idea spread that these patterns were *only* effective if hackled very sparsely. Actually, you can wind five or six turns of hackle around the post and produce a veritable cork of a dry fly that, with the application of a good floatant, will rival a Wulff in floating through riffles.

Although I still carry traditionally tied Adamses and a few Ginger Quills and the like, I now fish paraduns almost exclusively when working trout rising to duns. The simple truth is that these patterns will fool the more selective tailwater trout more often than traditional dry fly patterns.

Among pattern styles, paraduns are actually pretty uncontroversial with two exceptions. You will run into some delicious arguments on what color the wings should be. One school of thought says the wings should match those of the naturals, whereas the other school says it's more important to have highly visible wings (I like white poly, white turkey, or white calf body hair) so that you can see the strikes. I tend to split the difference and use the highly visible wings on my more general patterns, but if I'm imitating a specific dun, like a #18 Blue-Winged Olive that I know is common on tailwaters, I tie some pattterns that imitate the wing color of the natural as closely as possible.

The other exception has to do with the tails. The classic paradun pattern has forked tails usually made of hackle fibers. The forks are more imitative of the natural and are supposed to help float the fly in a more stable fashion. The difficulty with them is that they take a little longer to tie, break easily, and often get wrapped around the bend of the hook.

A few years ago a number of anglers came to the realization that a simple hackle-fiber tail, like those used in traditional dry-fly patterns, worked fine on parachute dry-fly patterns. If the flies were a little less stable, this was outweighed by another factor of significance. The straight hackle fibers, particularly if tied in with a little web, could represent a nymphal shuck to the rising trout.

This is important because trout key on the mayflies that appear to be caught or immobilized by the shuck they are emerging from—it's a slower moving, easier meal. This has led to a variety of shuck-type imitation tails on paraduns ranging from trimmed hackle to ostrich and even marabou. I now tie most of my paraduns with the simple hackle-fiber tails, but I do throw in a few standard forked tails and razzle-dazzle shuck tails for good measure.

EMERGERS

Probably the single most important fly fishing insight of the 1970s was the realization by anglers of what happens to mayflies, or any aquatic insect, in the inch or so of water below the surface when a hatch occurs and how this phenomenon affects trout behavior.

Fly fishermen began to note that a hatch of mayflies was not as simple as the nymphs swimming to the water's surface, shedding their nymphal shuck, and flying off into the sunset. During this process there were casualties. Some of the bugs were caught in the surface film, or more accurately the area of surface tension between water molecules at the river's surface, where they struggled to break through the tension and get on top of the water. Other nymphs were only partially formed and simply died in the surface film. Some found themselves caught in their nymphal shucks and unable to get out. Rather than a walk in the park, the hatch was a little more like getting stuck on the bad side of town—after dark.

Observant fly fishermen, who were in many cases trying to get an edge on selective tailwater trout, noted that the emerging nymphs and duns experiencing difficulties were preyed on relentlessly by the trout, particularly at the beginning of the hatch. A whole school of fishing emerging patterns has evolved. These patterns are considerably more effective for catching trout early on in the hatch than the dry-fly dun imitations.

I use several types of emerger patterns for fly fishing the tailwaters. I tie these patterns in the same colors I tie my duns and on the same sizes of hooks. I will admit a bit of prejudice toward the lighter-colored olives, tans, and dirty yellows for emergers, but you should still have some darker colors on hand.

Look for the trout to tip their hand when rising to emerger activity if the riseforms appear very deliberate and are occurring in narrow feeding lanes. This could indicate that they are taking crippled or stillborn nymphs. A porpoising head-to-tail rise might also be a clue. Another obvious giveaway is when a trout is rising but letting the hatched duns on the water's surface float right by him—untaken!

The two most effective emerger patterns are floating nymphs and quill-wing or hackle-tip emergers. I like floating nymph designs that have a relatively streamlined body and a hackle-tip tail that flares a bit to represent a shuck. What makes a floating nymph just that is a dubbed "wing ball" of polypropylene or other highly buoyant material that is tied in as a wing case. The wing ball lets the nymph float directly in the surface film where the trout take it as a nymph just before the shuck splits open or possibly as some sort of crippled nymph. Some tiers will add a parachute hackle wrapped around the ball although a good floatant will keep the unhackled rendition where you want it.

Other tiers use forked tails, which they believe help in flotation. That's up to you but I'd recommend that you experiment a little with trailing-shuck imitations that utilize ostrich, hackle fibers, and the like on this one. You'd be surprised at the response a bit of webby ostrich tied in as a tail elicits. Although some fly fishermen insist on a wing ball that matches the color of the emerging nymphs' wings, I draw the line on floating nymphs. They're hard enough to see when a little bit of white polypropylene is used for the ball. Why make it harder?

The quill-wing emerger uses mallard quill, hackle tips, or similar materials that are tied in short along the sides of the thorax of the fly. Tails and legs are best made of a soft material like partridge or mallard or wood-duck flank feathers. Under the right conditions these little stubs of wings seem to turn the trick on selectively rising trout. Both the floating nymph and quill-wing emerger should be fished using dry-fly techniques, although sometimes the trout will also nail the quill-wing emergers right at the beginning of the swing.

I'd be remiss if I didn't also mention that emerger patterns tied with soft hackles can also turn the trick during the early stages of the hatch. I am particularly fond of patterns that utilize marabou or the small down feathers found behind the regular flank feather on pheasant or partridge skins. A very simple fly with an olive-dubbed body and a hackle of down displays a tremendous amount of action that can be quite enticing to the trout.

You will find that the trout can be quite selective about the kind of emerger pattern they want. These patterns will get you in the ballpark most of the time but don't be afraid to modify any patterns, even including the paraduns, on the spot to gain the trout's attention.

My friend A. K. Best tells a story about a Blue-Winged Olive hatch he once fished where he couldn't figure out why the trout weren't accepting his offers. I have no doubt that his imitation was perfect. A. K. ties flies for a living and is the kind of guy who will dye quills in several layers of dyes just to get the colors perfect. I also know him to be a superlative caster of flies, so casting wasn't a problem.

It turned out that when he looked closely at the hatching flies, A. K. noticed that something was causing many of them to flop over on their sides as they emerged. He then promptly took his scissors and trimmed off all the hackle from one side of his paradun imitation so it would flop over on its side. He couldn't keep the trout away from his fly after that.

SPINNERS

You're also going to need some patterns to imitate the spent spinners that indicate the end game in the adult mayfly's life, when it falls after breeding with its wings spent flat out on the water's surface. Look for spinner falls, depending on mayfly species, either toward darkness in the evening or in the morning hours. Trout rising to spent spinners don't need to expend any energy in the chase, since their prey is already dead or close

Spinner imitations with polypropylene wings are easy to tie and effective.

to it, so their rises are thrifty to the point that in the failing light of the evening you may not even see them if you aren't looking for them.

In regard to patterns, I keep my spinners pretty basic. This is one pattern where I tie the hackle tails forked, although I've also just tied in standard, straight hackle-fiber tails that have worked fine. For the spent wings I most often use either white or dun-colored polypropylene. I make these wings a bit on the long side figuring that I can trim them shorter if necessary. I also carry some spinners tied with wings made of a traditionally wound hackle that I bunch together on either side of the hook to represent spent wings. These flies have a finer wing silhouette that may help when the trout are on the moody side.

Well-known fly tier Datus Proper introduced a spinner pattern tied specifically to imitate *Tricorythodes* a few years back that makes an effective spinner pattern for any of the smaller mayflies. He simply wraps the hackle over the front two-thirds of the hook shank, winds the body dubbing *through* it, then trims off the bottom of the hackle. This wispy sort of imitation works well on even the most selective trout.

When it comes to body colors for spinner patterns I am of the school that likes them a bit flashy, particularly for the lighter-colored flies. I

Fly Fishing the Tailwaters

A streamside fly tying kit may be required to tie specific patterns needed to fool very selective rising trout.

say this because these spinners often appear to have a kind of translucent quality on the water. To get the right effect I use one of the many brighter synthetic dubbing materials, like Fly Rite, that are now available. Rusty orange-browns for Pale Morning Duns, sparkly pale yellows for Pale Evening Duns, and even straight oranges for spent Hendricksons work well. Of course, I also carry black spinners in the small sizes for the Tricos, and several shades of nonflashy dubbed spinners in the darker shades ranging from chocolate brown to a grayish dun.

PATTERNS FOR PICKY TROUT

You certainly will run into those occasions now and then where a general fly pattern will not do. Tailwaters *are* known for this sort of thing and the best preparation for it is to carry a well-stocked portable fly-tying kit, particularly when traveling to a river that is new to you. My experience with very selective trout is that you can almost always land a few with *good presentations* of patterns that come close to representing the size and color of the naturals on the water. One tip is to stick to the emerger and floating nymph patterns if you're having a hard time. Ultimately, what the streamside tying kit will do for you is increase your percentages on the tough hatches. But remember, it's all based on your

No-hackle Compara-duns (right) sometimes turn the trick on finicky rising trout that refuse paraduns.

being able to determine what it is that is making those trout so selective and *that* isn't always so easy to figure out!

I do make some allowances for the possibility of trout being very selective to the species of mayflies that I figure I'm most likely to encounter, especially on the tailwaters with which I'm more familiar. I do this by tying quill-bodied paraduns to match Blue-Winged Olive hatches. I think the quill bodies, for whatever reason, will more often fool those hard-to-catch trout. I make a point to dye the quills so that their color closely matches that of the naturals that I most often see. I do the same for the Pale Morning Duns, which are a factor on many of the western tailwaters I most frequently fish. I make another concession on Trico spinner patterns that I tie on hooks as small as #24.

Finally, for good measure I carry a few no-hackle type dry-fly patterns for those trout that will take nothing else. I concentrate my tying efforts on the olives and dirty yellows but also throw in an occasional brown or tan. I still favor the Swisher-Richards No-Hackle Sidewinder tied with the matched duck feathers for wings for these no-hackle imitations, but even after a number of years I can't say I find them easy to tie. If you don't want to put up with tying the Sidewinders, a simple no-hackle paradun utilizing hen-tip wings and a little floatant will work. Al Caucci

Fly Fishing the Tailwaters

and Bob Nastasi's Compara-duns, as they explained them in their book *Hatches,* are also very effective no-hackle patterns for selective trout.

One final point on mayfly patterns. Many tailwater fisheries are very rich, to the point that not only do they have large populations of trout, but they have large populations of *large* trout. My friend Neill Peterson, who fishes the San Juan River on a regular basis, suggests that anglers consider using heavier wire hooks particularly on the small-size paradun patterns. Neill, who was using the standard 94840 Mustad dry-fly hooks that we all grew up on, has found himself turning to heftier numbers like the Mustad 3906 that many associate more with nymph patterns than dry flies. An extra wind of hackle and a touch of floatant allows paraduns tied on these heavier hooks to float well.

The heavier hooks help lessen the time that larger trout need to be played before being brought to net and also reduce the number of hooks straightened by husky trout. Other hook companies, notably Tiemco and Partridge, also offer heavier hooks that are workable for dry-fly patterns.

CADDISFLY IMITATIONS

The well-versed tailwater dry-fly fisherman will have to fill out his dry-fly arsenal with caddisfly imitations. Although caddisfly activity is hard to predict on many tailwaters, you can be assured that you will run into it. Some tailwaters, most notably in the East, are predominately caddis-fly waters, whereas other tailwaters may see only infrequent caddisfly activity where trout are actively rising.

I've gone through a number of caddisfly-tying phases but always find myself coming back to some rendition of Al Troth's venerable Elk Hair Caddis when these insects are dancing over the water. The pattern is relatively simple and consists of a wing of elk hair tied along the hook shank, a dubbed body, and a palmered hackle. Various renditions leave out the palmered hackle and add a collar hackle. Others have no hackles at all. I stick with the palmer-hackled jobs in hook sizes #18 through #14 and dubbed in body colors of tan, olive, gray, and black. I use wings that are bleached to a light tan, a darker mottled brown deer hair, and a very dark brown elk hair.

Not only do these patterns float like corks, but you can easily impart action to them by skittering, bouncing, or just letting them swing at the end of the drift. It is important to remember that caddis patterns, whatever your personal preference, often work best if they are given some sort of action.

A few other patterns that are fun to fool with during caddis hatches are either the Goddard Caddis or Humpy for faster water, various quill-winged numbers along the lines of the Henryville Special for flatter water, and maybe most importantly the good old traditionally tied Adams. The Adams is the one traditionally tied dry fly that I still use quite a bit on the tailwaters, and in many cases it's during a caddisfly hatch.

To be on the safe side you should have some sort of caddis emerger in your fly box. In the past I've gotten away with simple partridge soft-hackle patterns in the same body colors as my drys. Gary LaFontaine, who is the recognized authority on caddisflies, recommends imitating a number of stages of caddisfly development. Although I don't go that far, I have found his emergent, stubby-winged caddis patterns, which utilize a wispy overdubbing of Sparkle yarn to simulate the flashy air bubble that surrounds an emerging caddis, to be quite effective. They're really the only specialty caddisfly pattern I use.

A few pattern groups that represent terrestrial insects that find their way into tailwaters are a necessary addition to your fly box. Terrestrials for tailwater fly fishermen tend to be governed by local conditions. You can't go wrong with having some black ant, red ant, and deer-hair grasshopper patterns wherever you go. In the East, where terrestrials can be very important, you might also want some beetle patterns and some sort of inchworm pattern. Terrestrial patterns, like caddisfly patterns, are at times quite effective if a little action is imparted to the fly.

FLY PRESENTATION

Many tailwater anglers learned a hard lesson in the late 1960s and early 1970s. The perceived watchword then was that an exact match of any bug you might see or hope to see on the river would be your salvation for catching selective trout. I say "perceived" because those professional anglers who were writing and lecturing about matching naturals were also talking about fly presentation. It's just that most of us weren't listening because we were too busy tying flies.

Actually, there's a bit of historical precedent for it. It seems that as a rule, Americans have always been more intrigued by the idea of finding *the* cosmic fly rather than attaining the perfect drift or the perfect cast. The Europeans, particularly on the Continent, seem to be just the opposite. There you find one casting club after another. It's been said that Charles Ritz used only a #14 Tupps Indispensible for twelve years!

The point, as we've known all along, is that you need both. A less than perfect fly that is superbly presented will probably make for a very good day of fishing. An accurate match coupled with a superb cast and drift does occasionally occur and it is simply sheer ectasy.

I'm not a superlative caster but over time I've learned a few tricks that have helped me catch rising trout. The most important thing you will ever learn about casting to rising trout is to throw slack. Casting all those S-curves may not be pretty, but it's that slack line that allows your dry fly or emerger pattern to drift in a natural fashion over the trout.

There are a number of ways to get slack into the line. Most commonly, a little horizontal quiver is imparted to the rod just as the line straightens on the forecast. You can also stop the rod abruptly on the forecast, which causes curves to form in the line and leader when the rod bounces back a bit. The leader also can be "piled" by dropping the tip of the rod just before the leader turns over on the forecast.

Like anything else that goes with fly fishing, you can pursue presentation as deeply as you want to. I know anglers who spend as much time designing leaders as they do tying flies and I know others who have a special rod for every conceivable casting situation.

Positioning yourself for the most advantageous cast is equally important as presentation. Traditionally, dry flies have been presented from downstream of the rising trout. In this way the fly can drift, drag free, for a relatively long period of time if the angler has positioned himself so no other currents disrupt the fly's drift. As the fly floats downstream with the current the angler simply gathers up the slack line on the water.

An added advantage of the downstream position is that the trout, which are feeding with their heads facing into the current, can be approached without being alerted to the angler's presence. The difficulty with a presentation from the downstream position is that the caster must figure his distances accurately or risk either spooking or "lining" the trout if his cast is too long and the trout is frightened off by the fly line or heavier parts of the leader.

An across-stream presentation can be used, but casting across currents of differing speeds will cause line drag to develop rapidly. Longer rods help in across-stream casts, where they can be used to mend line and keep line off the water. A reach cast, where the line is thrown out above the fly by a quick upstream motion of the fly rod at the end of the cast, can buy you an extended drag-free drift in cross-stream casting situations if the water isn't moving too fast.

The best casting position to be in is upstream from the rising trout. The approach must be made with caution and must stop at a distance where the trout will not be spooked. It's best not to position yourself in the drift lane directly above the rising fish because any disturbance you cause to the streambed will be carried right over the trout by the current and might spook them. Try to position yourself just off the main line of the drift. When you cast, be sure to throw some slack line. You can also feed line out from the reel if the cast is too short. The primary advantages of the presentation from upstream are that your fly is the first thing the trout sees and you can maintain a drag-free drift for a considerably longer period of time. When using the downstream cast, take special care not to spook the trout when lifting unaccepted presentations off the water for another cast.

No matter from what position you make your presentation, it's important to make a quiet, nondisruptive approach to it. Take a few minutes to observe the rising trout and plan your approach. Walk quietly along the stream bank and enter the water with as little commotion as possible, then wade carefully into position.

I always try to assess how spooky I think the trout will be. If I'm working up to a pod of risers in six inches of flat, gin-clear backwater, I'm going to be a lot more delicate than if that same pod of fish is working the tongue of current that's fanning out at the head of a pool. Sometimes you must assume a crouching or even kneeling position if trout are feeding in a sensitive lie. It will also pay to be aware of where your shadow falls on the water.

Fly Fishing the Tailwaters

The important thing to remember in your approach is that the closer you can position yourself to the rising trout without alarming them, the better your chances of success will be. I always figure that the shorter the cast, the less there is that can go wrong. Shorter casts have less chance of putting line into a mishmash of currents that are bound to cause drag. Shorter casts have less chance of accidentally hitting the water too hard. Shorter casts are more likely to be accurate. With practice you'll be surprised how close you can get to rising trout.

Once you have made your approach and are in casting position it is generally best to pick a single rising trout on which to concentrate. The way the trout is rising will tell you a lot about what it's feeding on. A dimpling rise usually indicates the fish is feeding on emergent insect forms just at the point where they are metamorphosing into the winged forms and are vulnerable. Splashy rises indicate the trout may be chasing a swimming nymph or slashing the surface for a winged mayfly attempting to get into the air. Any number of bulging or gulping riseforms may ruffle the surface if the trout are taking stillborn or crippled duns or spent spinners. In many cases trout rising to spent spinners are barely discernable, with only their snouts gently breaking the water's surface.

How far you put the fly above the rising trout will depend on a number of technical factors mostly related to getting a drag-free drift. Assess the current speed and then decide what you have to do in the way of mending line. As a rule I don't usually cast the fly much more than a foot or two above the trout I've singled out unless there are extenuating circumstances. I also figure that the more selective a trout is, the less likely it will move sideways, upstream, or downstream to take an artificial. This means casts have to be right on its nose. Your saving grace here is that if you've managed to approach the trout fairly closely and don't froth up the water on your casts, odds are good you'll get at least a couple of chances before you put the fish down.

Fishing the tailwater hatches can do it to you. The trout can be maddeningly selective one day and then just picky the next. They can be tough, especially on tailwaters that are subject to heavy fishing pressure. That's when you'll need it all—the right fly patterns, good approaches and presentations, drag-free drifts, and a bit of luck. If that doesn't work, throw in a little razzle-dazzle.

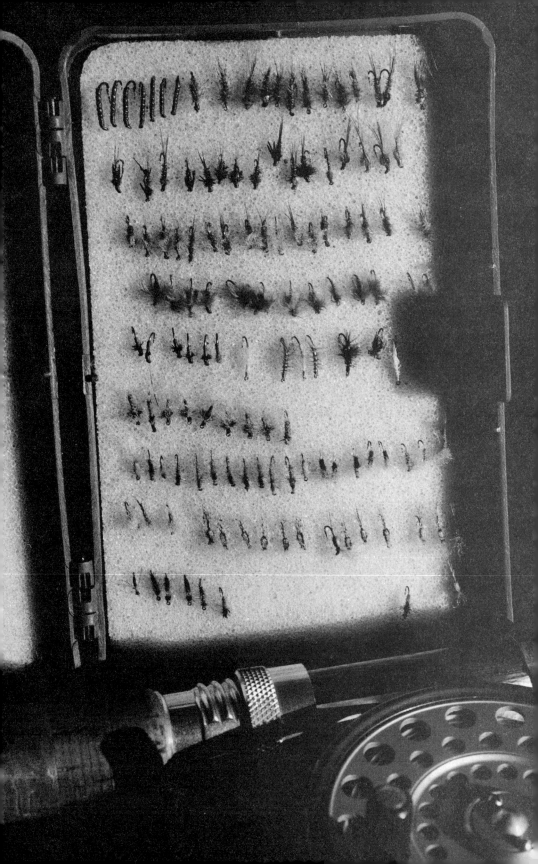

CHAPTER 6

The Champagne of Tailwater Angling–
Fishing the Midges

A S MUCH AS ANYTHING, the anglers will clue you in to the midge hatch. You will see them hunched over in concentration like herons. The better ones will be in as close as they can get to the dimpling trout. What you'll notice is the rhythmic flicking of casts toward the porpoising trout and the lack of any other motions. The only exception will be the gentle tug that sets a very small hook attached to the leader by a very delicate tippet. The playing of the trout, if it is a good one, will be a sweet cat-and-mouse sort of ecstasy.

If you're interested in a little ecstasy when it comes to fly fishing the tailwaters, you will become a midge fisherman. Midges are a factor in most tailwaters, and in the colder tailwaters their impact on the trout's diet takes on added importance. While a single midge may range any-where in length from a tiny 3 millimeters to what amounts to a giant specimen at 6 millimeters, their value to the trout revolves not so much around individuals as it does around populations.

In many tailwaters midges can hatch at any hour during the day, any month of the year, and the hatches can go on for hours at a time if not for an entire day. What the midges lack in size they make up for in num-bers. This ready availability and quantity of midges on a tailwater is what makes them so important.

The tiny flies that we call "midges" actually cover a broad range of families found in the insect order Diptera. A characteristic of Dipterans is that they are two-winged flies. Other common trout foods such as mayflies, caddisflies, and stoneflies have two *pairs* of wings as adults. Members of Diptera also have what is referred to as a complete metamorphosis that consists of egg, larval, pupal, and adult stages.

Midges are known to many fly fishermen as those insects occupying sections of tailwaters directly below the deep, bottom-release reservoirs where very cold water is discharged. In some cases the midges are the only insects hardy enough to be found in reliable numbers in those areas immediately below the dams, although their populations will also prosper for quite a few miles downstream.

Anglers often associate very large populations of midges with the relatively constant flows of water released from water-storage reservoirs. The constant water flow rates from these reservoirs allow for the growth of aquatic vegetation. This vegetation is advantageous to many species of midges, particularly those in the family Chironomidae, which is well represented in many tailwaters. Sections of slower water, with a silty or fine-grained sand bottom, also provide suitable habitat for many species of midges.

While these conditions are ideal for the production of very large populations of midges, it should be noted that good populations of midges can also be found in the tailwaters below many hydroelectric facilities. The members of Diptera are amazingly tough. It has been noted by researchers that midge populations appear to be able to survive for some time when stranded out of the water by the fluctuations of flow rates associated with the generation of power.

Fishing midge imitations has certainly gained its fair market share of the mythology, hocus-pocus, media hype, and all those other things that slide into the fly fishing scene on occasion. When everything is said and done, midging is really only as hard as you make it. One thing is definite: it certainly is not as enigmatic as many of the mayfly hatches you will try to figure out. You can also reason that with the midges being so widespread and prolific in the tailwaters you *will* get your licks in. By developing a couple of new skills and discarding a few outdated perceptions, you'll be holding your own as a midger in no time.

Tailwater trout feed on midges during the larval, pupal, and adult

Midge larva imitations are usually fished using dead drift nymphing techniques.

stages of their development. In practice, tailwater anglers are most apt to ignore fishing imitations of the wormlike larval stage. This is probably because fishing the larval stage of midges just isn't as exciting as fishing the pupal or adult stages. But that doesn't mean you shouldn't consider it. Midge imitations of the larval stage can be fished using standard dead drift nymphing techniques, and as an added incentive you can often use imitations tied on somewhat larger and stouter hooks.

TYING AND FISHING
MIDGE LARVA IMITATIONS

I'm like a lot of other anglers when it comes to dead drifting midge larva imitations. I usually end up tying on a midge larva imitation when my other standard nymphs haven't turned the trick. The fact is, I don't often set out to fish larva imitations unless I know that they are important in a particular tailwater or unless certain conditions exist that make me think the larva have become a factor. I consider any kind of disturbance in the water flows as a good reason to put on a larva imitation. A change in water discharge rates from the reservoir will sometimes knock midge

The best midge imitations are small, simply tied flies. Shown clockwise from the top are: biot midge larva, midge pupa hackled with a partridge down feather, Larva Lace midge larva, midge larva (in the center), and floating midge pupa with splayed hackle tail representing a shuck.

larva into the drift, and since populations of midge larva can be astronomical in some tailwaters, this can mean a real feeding orgy will occur.

Just because *I* don't always concentrate on midge larva doesn't mean they aren't a factor. I remember one early season on the South Platte River when every time I came across Bruce Stagg he was fishing a little #20 Miracle Nymph. This popular and simple imitation consists of a body of white floss ribbed with copper wire. The floss added some flash to the fly and I don't know whether the trout were taking it as a larva that had somehow accidentally found itself in the drift, or perhaps as a pupa that was just beginning to move to the surface. All I know is it seemed like Bruce always had a fish on, even when there was no sign of midge activity on or near the surface.

The Miracle Nymph brings out a couple of important points about tying midge imitations. First of all, midge imitations, whether they represent the larval, pupal, or adult stage, are always quite simple ties. Their most complicated manifestations amount to little more than a trace of dubbing for the body and a wisp of hackle. Many pupa and larva imi-

Fly Fishing the Tailwaters

tations consist solely of a little colored dubbing on a hook.

Secondly, white can be an effective color for midge larva imitations. Another popular larva imitation called the String Thing is often tied in white or off-white colors. The String Thing is as simple to tie as winding a strand of buttonhole thread around the shank of a hook.

I don't know why the whites work, but it isn't hard to figure out why other important larva colors like red or orange do. You can find midge larva in these colors just by rooting around on the stream bottom. An effective larva pattern representing these colors can be tied using the translucent shades of red, orange, and amber available in Larva Lace. Black and olive are two more good basic colors for your larva imitations.

Another excellent material for tying larva patterns is goose biot dyed in a variety of colors. The biot is simply wound around the hook shank and the fly is finished with a collar of peacock or ostrich herl. Since midge larva are so easy to tie, it won't hurt to round out your larva imitations with any other colors that tickle your fancy.

One aspect of actually fishing the larva imitations that can make it difficult is that the trout tend to hug the stream bottom when they feed on the larva and seldom move even a hair to take an imitation. You will have a better chance of success with larva-feeding trout if you can sight-fish to them. If you can see the trout, you can track where your imitation is drifting and work to get it right on the trout's nose, greatly increasing your chances of a take.

TERMINAL TACKLE AND FLY RODS FOR MIDGE FISHERMEN

The terminal tackle necessary for dead drifting midge larva imitations doesn't have to differ radically from your standard dead drift nymphing rig other than the necessity for finer tippets in the 5X to 7X range. Fine tippets, besides being necessary just to get them through the small eyes of the hooks (I don't often find it necessary to get much smaller than a #18 or #20 hook in long-shank styles for larva imitations), also impart an action to the fly that the trout find stimulating.

There *are* terminal tackle refinements that some midgers find helpful, whether they are fishing deep or at the water's surface. This is especially true when it comes to landing trout on the finer tippets and smaller hooks required for midging. Most commonly, you will find midgers using the braided leaders now available. The argument for the braided leader is that it adds more stretch to the leader system than can be accomplished by just adding extra length to the finer-size tippets, which is the traditional way that midgers have gotten more stretch and thus more pound-test for their money.

Other high-tech midgers may add bungy cord material either within a braided leader or between the fly line and the monofilament leader. The bungy cord adds considerable stretch to the system and can make the difference on very large trout caught on delicate terminal tackle, particularly in terms of the time it takes to bring the fish to net.

If you decide to stick to the more traditional terminal tackle, especially when fishing pupa-stage or adult-stage midge imitations, remember that a thirty-inch to forty-inch tippet of 7X or 8X material really will add to the relative pound-test of your line because it will stretch more than a twelve-inch or eighteen-inch tippet of the same material. For dead drifting you'll usually have to live with a somewhat shorter tippet, because an extremely long tippet can make casting and strike detection difficult. Also note that the most vulnerable areas in your entire leader system are the blood knot between your tippet and leader and the knot at the fly, which is best tied with an improved clinch knot.

Once you start running with the midge fishermen, the one other item of equipment, besides terminal gear, that you will endlessly hear about is the classic dry-fly midging rod. This can be anything from a 6-foot cane affair for a 4-weight line to one of the new graphite rods designed for a 2-weight line. Lightness seems to be the watchword among the midgers. Any of these lightweight numbers can be fine midging rods but they aren't absolutely necessary. I fished midge imitations for years with a stout 9-foot Fisher Kennedy graphite rod designed for a 6-weight line. It got the job done just fine.

Whether you *want* a special midging rod is a whole different story. I think the midges are a wonderful reason to get on the horn and talk to a builder of high-quality cane rods like Mike Clark and say, "Why don't you build me something for the midges, say in a five weight, that will

Fly Fishing the Tailwaters

have enough backbone to carry me through the rest of the day down on the South Platte." I think I'd probably draw the line at getting something so light or so short that it would become mandatory that I carry another nymphing rod for a day's excursion on the river. The one comment I have heard when it comes to cane rods and the very light graphite rods is that some anglers feel they break fewer fish off using these softer-action rods.

FISHING THE INITIAL STAGE OF MIDGE PUPA EMERGENCE

If you spend enough time watching trout take midge larva while they hug the bottom, sooner or later you will observe an important aspect of the midge hatch and the way the trout respond to it. This is the initial stage of pupation. During this brief stage in the midge's life cycle it is most available to the trout as it rises toward the water's surface and then sheds its pupal shuck in the surface film on its way to the winged adult stage.

You can detect when the pupa are just beginning to rise from the bottom toward the surface by the trout's behavior. Initially, they too will begin to rise a little from the bottom, by just a few inches, while continuing to feed. You will also observe the occasional trout flashing in the drift. As the emergence continues, the trout will suspend in the drift at varying levels between the surface and the stream bottom. Finally, the action will shift to the surface film, where you'll see the first evidence of activity on the surface when the trout begin to dimple as they take the pupa.

The period of time between the beginning of the emergence and actual observation of surface activity in the form of dimpling can be anywhere from thirty minutes to several hours and often goes unnoticed by anglers who are keyed to surface activity. Midgers who do pick up on this more subtle period of occasional flashes and trout slowly suspending themselves higher and higher up in the drift are sometimes in for some of the best midging of the hatch.

Although you will get strikes if you continue to dead drift larva imitations during the initial phases of pupation, you will be best served by dead drifting pupa imitations or a dropper system with a larva imitation closest to the weight and a pupa as the point fly. It's best to seine the drift to get an idea of the color and size of the emerging midges, but in a pinch I'd put on a pupa imitation in an olive shade in the #20 to #22 hook-size range. You'll be surprised how many of the tailwater pupa fall into this color range, especially during the initial phases of pupation. Again, most pupa imitations are easy to tie, so you might as well carry them in a range of colors including black, gray, amber, dirty yellow, tan, and white.

My favorite all-around pattern to imitate this early subsurface stage of pupation is dubbed in an appropriate color of dyed rabbit with no guard hairs and hackled with the soft down feather found *behind* the Hungarian partridge flank feather used in standard soft-hackle nymphs. Down feathers of the same kind but in somewhat larger sizes can be found on ring-necked pheasant skins. Because the quill of the down feather is extremely delicate, it takes a bit of practice to be able to wind it hackle fashion around the hook shank. You'll find that it's worth the trouble. The down gives a seductive, lifelike breathing quality to the fly. It also creates a close imitation of the gills found on many of the naturals, especially the Chironomids.

You need to fine tune your terminal tackle and dead drift nymphing technique to fish this initial part of the pupal stage most effectively. First of all, lengthen your tippet to twenty-five or even thirty inches of 5X to 7X material below the weight. The fine tippet material coupled with the longer length of tippet between the weight and the fly will allow the pupa imitation to well up naturally with the current in a fashion similar to the emerging midges. Cast this rig upstream and allow it to dead drift with the current. At the end of the dead drift let the imitation swing with the current and rise to the surface. In many cases the trout will take it on the swing. Another variation is to quarter the cast upstream. Once the imitation has reached the stream bottom on the dead drift, slowly raise the rod tip to imitate the emerging pupa.

Once on the Frying Pan River I used these techniques to engage a memorable trout. I had visually located a pod of three trout that were tucked in close to the bank and suspended up in the current while feeding steadily on pupa. The fish were large. Getting a good dead drift to them was virtually impossible due to a current created by water from an incoming spring. I couldn't even get the drifts close enough to the trout to spook them. After a lot of experimentation, I finally found that if I cast perfectly to a small dead spot between the bank and the incoming spring water I could get just enough of a dead drift to put the fly in front of the trout before the current caused it to drag.

I tied on a wonderful imitation that Roy Palm had thought up. It was a white marabou-bodied number tied with a Flashabou rib on a long-shank #20 hook. The trout took it on the first cast where I got the drift right and proceeded to take me downtown. When it was over I'd landed a $5\frac{1}{2}$-pound cutthroat with a #20 imitation on a 6X tippet.

At that time, I was using a nymphing rig that included a braided leader with a bungy-cord insert. I think that's the only way I could have landed the fish, which was very strong. It was the kind of trout that when the time came to take the hook out and release him my hands were shaking. That nymphing situation had every element of high adventure that I've ever come across in the most delicate dry-fly situations.

FISHING LATE STAGES OF MIDGE PUPA EMERGENCE

Eventually the trout will nudge their way into the surface film as they follow the emerging midges, and another change in tactics will be required. This is the best-known phase of the hatch among midge fishermen, although anglers new to the game often mistake the dimpling rises for trout feeding solely on adult midges. While the trout will take adults during this phase, closer observation will reveal that they are feeding predominantly on pupa suspended in the surface film or adults that are on the surface but not yet completely out of their pupal shucks. Along with the dimpling, or as the English say, "smutting," rise you will probably see trout performing a head-to-tail porpoising rise where they stay in the same place in the drift but rhythmically rise, head to tail, while taking pupa.

When you're new to midging you tend to notice all of this surface activity in the flatter sections of water. Prime spots are at the head of a pool where the current fans out, at the tail of a pool, and more sporadically over the length and breadth of a pool. Although many species of midges emerge from the calmer water with the appropriate stream bottom, don't limit your search for trout rising to midges

A slack-line downstream cast can be very effective when the trout are rising to midges.

to just the flats, pools, and backwaters. Long, gentle riffles are often the scene of superlative midge hatches.

Several aspects of the dimpling trout's behavior are important to note before you ever make a cast. You must realize that these midges are coming off the water in incredible numbers and that, at least in the initial phases of the hatch, the trout are taking predominantly the pupal form, which is quite vulnerable. What this means is that the midging trout are going to stick very closely to their feeding lanes—probably to the degree that they won't move even an inch to take an artificial! You will also observe that individual trout will develop definite feeding rhythms. Both types of behavior provide for a metabolic thriftiness on the trout's part.

For the midge feeding equation to work out, a trout needs to balance the energy it expends taking the midges against the energy it receives by eating them. The narrow feeding lanes and rhythmical feeding movements, which utilize the river's energy almost exclusively to propel the trout through its feeding motions, are what keep the trout in the black, so to speak. The midge fisherman, like any good trout broker, needs to work with these behaviors, always keeping an eye on the trends.

Enough "trout market" talk. The question is, how do you catch midg-

Fly Fishing the Tailwaters

ing trout? Your casting position is important. I tend to split the difference, depending on several factors, between casting from an upstream position and casting from a more traditional downstream position. If I'm looking at a lot of risers in, say, a big long glide, my tendency is to get as close as possible to the rising trout in a downstream and somewhat across stream position. You want to be as close as you can get so that you can keep as much fly line off the water (and out of disruptive, drag-producing crosscurrents) as possible. If I can keep *all* of the line off the water by holding the rod a little higher and making short casts, it's all the better. This down-and-across position allows you to make a lot of casts and catch a lot of trout before you put all of them down.

A variation is to fish directly across stream from the risers, if you can get close enough or in a good enough position to not be fighting drag on every cast. Another option is to approach the trout from upstream and slightly across stream. This is the preferred position for casting to smaller pods of trout and for working monster fish where you want all the odds in your favor. The advantages are the same as for a dry fly presented from an upstream position. It is easier to control the drift and possible drag on the pupa imitation, and the imitation is the first thing that the trout sees. The disadvantage is that you are more likely to put the trout down when lifting the fly off the water, which means the first cast must be well planned and on the money.

MIDGE PUPA IMITATIONS FOR FISHING THE SURFACE FILM

The question of selectivity in midging trout is an interesting one. My experience has been that midging trout don't seem to be selective as often as trout rising to mayflies. You still need to be in the ballpark on your pupa selection, but figure on a little more leeway in most situations. I have a number of pet pupa imitations that I use in many midging situations. All these patterns reflect certain characteristics that I like in midge pupa imitations and they all include marabou or down feathers because of the action they impart to the flies.

Other critical patterns for the surface film include representations of trailing shucks made either of cut hackle tips or polypropylene. These can be as simple as a "tail" of polypropylene trailed behind a hook dubbed in an appropriate shade of rabbit fur, or you can add a dubbed wing ball like you find on floating nymphs. Some tiers even include tiny hackle-point or duck-shoulder feather wings on the sides of the imitations. My policy on pupa imitations is to keep them simple. It's better to have a box full of extra flies than too few perfect but hard-to-tie imitations. You *will* lose these flies to the trout on a regular basis. That's just a fact of the midger's life.

A final pupa pattern that you shouldn't be without is called the Kimball's Emerger after its creator Mike Kimball. This little fly consists of a dubbed polypropylene thorax in a range of colors, a tail of teal flank tied splayed to represent a trailing shuck, and a wing case of polypropylene tied in a small loop that is humped up in the back but tapered toward the eye of the hook. This fly has no abdomen, so that the body occupies only the first third or half of the hook shank behind the eye. In terms of what the trout perceive, "short shanking" the fly this way in effect gives you a smaller fly, but one tied on a hook large enough so that it improves your fish hooking and fish holding capacities.

When it comes to selecting the pupa imitation for any particular midging situation, the first thing I do is try to get an approximate fix on color. Size is the next consideration and there are two schools of thought among midgers on this. You can either match the size of the natural as closely as possible or do what I do and start off with a #20 or #22 pupa imitation no matter what size the naturals are. Even though not matching size is heresy to many fly fishermen, I don't when fishing midges for several reasons. The first is a practical consideration—I've found that my ability to hook, hold, and land fish drops off radically when I use hook sizes smaller than #22. I've also found that in many midging situations the trout may actually be more sensitive to your presentation than to the exact size of the fly.

It could also be that in a typical midge hatch there are a number of size ranges represented in the surface film and on top of the water. There are midges trailing variously sized shucks and midges that have their wings splayed in unusual ways. You will even see clumps consisting of numerous midges floating down the river. For all these reasons, why not start off with the increased hooking capabilities of a larger hook? It may be all that is necessary and if it isn't you can always drop a hook size or so.

I'll admit that while I still carry #26 pupa imitations in my fly box, they are left over from years ago when catching trout on #26 and #28 hooks was one of the ways we proved our manhood. I can't remember the last time I used them but I keep them there for those occasions when someone asks, "What kind of man are you?" That's when I show them the #26 midge pupa imitations.

SKILLS FOR FISHING MIDGE PUPA IMITATIONS

When you start out fishing midge pupa imitations there are a few things you will have to get used to. At least in the beginning, give yourself as many advantages as you can. Rather than trying to work the risers that are coming up out in the middle of a shallow, mirrorlike flat, set your sights on those risers that are working the head of a pool where the incoming current puts a bit of a ruffle on the water's surface. Any slight disturbance on the water's surface will help to hide your leader and cover up any casting mistakes you might make. I've found that trout midging in these areas can actually be pretty forgiving if you're not slapping the water too badly or allowing your fly line to drag across the feeding lanes.

Once you've positioned yourself to cast to the smutting trout, you need to pick a fish on which to concentrate your efforts. A hatch of midges on a rich tailwater can result in fifty or sixty or even a hundred trout rising from bank to bank in the flats and glides. It may seem that just a cast out into the mass of them is good enough, but in most cases it makes hookups more difficult.

There are several reasons why. First of all, a midging trout will seldom break its feeding rhythm to take your presentation. If you study one trout and time your cast to coincide with its feeding rhythm you increase your odds of a take.

Secondly, midging trout are notorious for sticking to their feeding lanes. You need to put your cast right on the nose of the trout at the right time if you want to get a response. By making accurate casts to individual fish you increase your odds of a take over just casting willy-nilly into the risers and hoping that you are "on."

Finally, your midge pupa imitations are so small that, unlike a standard dry-fly imitation, you won't be able to see them on the water. Knowing where your fly is on the water takes some getting used to and a bit of practice. If you make your casts to trout you have targeted you should at least know the general area that your fly is in even if you can't see it.

Knowing the location of the pupa imitation is often a stumbling block for beginning midgers. In some ways it's a lot like detecting strikes when nymphing—with practice and perseverence you eventually get the hang of it. You can make it easier on yourself by getting as close to the rising trout as possible. That takes a lot of the mystery out of it because you have a better chance of tracking the fly.

A take is often no different than the dimpling rises around it, so you need to concentrate. It sometimes helps to use pupa imitations that have a bit of white polypropylene in them, like the Kimball's Emerger. In some cases you may be able to see this imitation on the water if there isn't much foam. Try to avoid sidearm casts that may throw a curve in your leader and stick to leaders with stiff butt sections that cast straighter.

In midging situations it's often best to put your cast just a few inches or so upstream of the dimpling trout. Long drifts aren't necessary and just make it harder to track the fly. It's safe to assume that you will make more casts per trout when midging than in most other surface or surface-film feeding situations. It's easy to mistake this for extreme selectivity to pattern rather than extreme selectivity to presentation. Before you start changing flies every cast, remember that these trout are essentially feeding with blinders on. Presentations made even slightly out of their feeding lanes won't be accepted.

Concentrate your efforts on getting the fly where it needs to be. If the trout still aren't taking but you are satisfied that your presentations have been accurate, then change flies, possibly to a smaller size, and work for casting accuracy again. Remember, your imitation has to be in the water to catch fish. If you're spending too much time fiddling around changing imitations, you will have less time to work on making accurate presentations.

Fly Fishing the Tailwaters

Generally speaking, a drag-free drift is the best way to present the pupa, although you might want to occasionally add a twitch or two of action to the imitation. Sometimes allowing the fly to swing at the end of the drift will induce a random take, too.

HOOKING AND PLAYING TROUT ON FINE TIPPETS

Okay, let's say everything falls into place and after the mandatory fifteen or twenty casts you put the pupa exactly where it has to be. As it drifts over the trout you notice that almost imperceptible tension in the leader and suddenly realize you have a fish on. Instinctively you put the graphite to the trout. You then note that it doesn't take long for the flyless leader to drift back down to earth after having rocketed toward to sky. You also find that you have either broken the fish off right at the fly or where the tippet was tied to the leader. Finally, you sigh and say to yourself that you know better than that. You simply can't put it to a #22 midge pupa on the end of a 7X tippet like you can to a Muddler Minnow on a 3X tippet. How about that?

It happens to everyone, that's just part of midging. What you can hope for is that it will happen less as you get more and more comfortable with the light tippets and small flies.

When it comes to hooking trout, think of it just that way; forget the word "strike." You're a midge fisherman, not a fighter pilot. You can get ample penetration with the small needlelike hooks used for midge flies by gently lifting the rod tip. Some anglers lift the rod while releasing their line hand altogether. I don't recommend that because you could end up with an unmanageable line situation if the trout takes off. Try making a circle with your thumb and forefinger like the traditional "okay" signal with your line hand when hooking fish. Just the fly line dragging through the guides will hook the trout and your line hand will be in position if you need it. With practice, and probably the heartbreak of a number of breakoffs, you'll learn what works best for you. Remember, it is a *gentle* art.

Hooking the trout isn't the end of it, either. The fish still needs to be brought to net. If you've hooked the trout in slow-moving water, you can

Trout hooked on the light terminal tackle and small flies required when midging are most often lost right as they are being netted.

drop the rod tip if you need to decrease line pressure on the fish. This will tend to calm the trout. By raising the rod tip a little and increasing pressure slowly by increments you make the trout work a little harder and eventually tire it out. If the trout makes a run, drop the rod tip to reduce line pressure. For playing fish in faster currents, the rod tip must be held high to keep excess line off the water where it's a source of drag. This extra resistance is likely to spook the trout, which can result in breakoffs.

Trout hooked on light terminal tackle are most commonly lost just as they are brought to the net. It's very easy to find out at this point that the trout you thought you'd worn out has gotten a second wind. With all of your line on the reel and the rod held high over your head as you bring the fish to net, all you really have between you and a free-swimming trout is a very tightly stretched 6X or 7X tippet. Needless to say, this is a delicate time. Don't make sudden movements. Bring the net in from behind the trout where it is hidden from the trout's view. If the trout does make a run, get the rod tip down as quickly as possible and throw slack if necessary.

It's kind of a contradiction, but I should say that it's best if you can land these trout as quickly as possible. From a practical standpoint, the

Fly Fishing the Tailwaters

quicker you get the fish in, the less chance there is that something will go wrong and you'll lose it. From a conservation viewpoint, remember that trout that have been tired by an excessively long battle on light terminal tackle may be a survival risk, particularly if water temperatures are high. Be sure to fully revive these trout before releasing them back into the river. There's no doubt that while you're learning the ins and outs of fishing midge imitations you will overplay your catches before you bring them to net. Once you get into the swing of things you'll be surprised how strong a thirty-inch tippet of 6X or 7X really is and your playing time will go down.

ADULT STAGE MIDGES

There is a final phase in the midge's life cycle that can provide the midger with fascinating trouting. Although trout often feed heavily on midge pupa, especially at the beginning of the hatch, they almost always take any adults that drift through their feeding lanes, too. As a hatch progresses trout will sometimes switch to feeding primarily on adult midges. A number of years ago, before I realized that many of the dimples I was seeing during a midge hatch represented fish feeding on pupa, I fished exclusively with dry flies. I used a variety of imitations ranging from little #24 palmer-hackled numbers to tiny Ginger Quill imitations tied without wings to patterns as simple as a thread body with a few turns of hackle on a #26 hook. I also included the classic Griffith's Gnat with its peacock body and grizzly hackle tied palmer style. The Griffith's Gnat was tied to imitate the clumps of midges that sometimes include a dozen or more flies floating on the water's surface.

You can use basic dry-fly techniques when presenting adult midge imitations. In some cases, if the light is just right and there isn't much foam or debris on the water's surface, these tiny drys might actually be visible. The sight of a tiny fly disappearing into the middle of a dimple can result in a tippet-popping response, so try to keep the buck fever in check on those somewhat rare occasions when conditions allow you to see your fly. As was also the case with trout rising to midge pupa, it pays to establish a casting position as close as possible to trout that are rising to adult forms of midges. The close-in positioning helps quicken your response time to takes, makes management of slack line easier, and offers visual cues to takes that you might not pick up if you're casting from farther away.

When you tie your adult imitations, make it a point to have both dark-colored and some light-colored imitations. Very bright reds, yellows, and oranges sometimes turn the trick, too. It might also pay to have a few experimental numbers that include a trailing shuck of some sort. Stillborns, tied to imitate midge pupa that didn't manage to get out of the shuck alive, can be very effective patterns since trout tend to key on these vulnerable forms. Dry flies that have a hackle at both the front and rear can be used to imitate mating midges.

Although you can usually depend on midge pupa imitations to be productive throughout the hatch, don't forget your adult patterns especially if the action slows. Sometimes all it takes is to switch from pupa imitations over to the dry-fly patterns. It's particularly important to keep an open mind when fishing to trout that are rising to the adult forms of midges. If one kind of presentation doesn't work, try another; if you've tried a certain fly pattern for a while and it fails to move the fish, switch patterns. If a trout doesn't take a fly put right on its nose, try casting it a couple of feet above the fish and letting it drift down to it. Midging trout can be finicky and it pays to try as many alternatives on them as you can think of.

I look for the best midging to occur on the cloudy, cooler days. The hatches on cloudy days, like most aquatic insect hatches, seem longer and more prolific. The cooler weather also seems to slow down the pupa's emergence from the shuck a bit, which means that it is on the water and available to the trout a little longer.

Some of the very best fishing I've experienced on the tailwaters has been to midging trout. The rise to these tiny two-winged flies can have many faces. It might be that one day you can't do anything wrong but the next you work feverishly over dozens and dozens of dimpling trout to absolutely no avail.

The biggest surprise of all is when you discover at the end of your line how enormous some of these midging trout are. It might be that all you *see* is a little bigger than average dorsal fin porpoising rhythmically in the current as you line up your cast. Maybe you don't think twice

about it until the line tightens up all of a sudden and this pickup truck rolls over in the current. You are in for the most delicate dance of your angling life if you want to land that trout. And if you do, you will know all about the champagne of tailwater angling.

It can come in some pretty big bottles.

Fall or spring spawning runs can add a new dimension to the tailwater angler's season.

CHAPTER 7

Special Cases and Curiosities

ALONG WITH THE ENIGMA of the mayfly and caddisfly hatches, the tricky predictability of the midges, and the almost certain nymphing possibilities, the tailwaters provide a few angling twists you may not find anywhere else.

WINTER TAILWATER FISHING

Among the special cases, it is the year-round fly fishing possibilities in many tailwaters that fly fishermen find the most delightful. It seems that a number of tailwaters find themselves in the hallowed company of spring creeks and those rivers that remain open year-round because of geothermal effects. Where fishing regulations permit, particularly in the western states, tailwaters have become a refuge for winter-weary fly fishermen suffering the effects of cabin fever.

The reason that many deep-release tailwaters do remain open during the cold months goes back to the way in which the thermal regimen of the river is altered below the dam. It's the old winter warm and summer cool conditions so often encountered when studying the water temperatures below these deep-release reservoirs.

What happens is that the somewhat warmer water being released from the reservoir, coupled with a fairly constant water flow rate, is usually enough to keep a tailwater open for at least a couple of miles downstream from the dam. The exact length of the area of open water is, of course, dependent on a number of factors such as air temperatures, the

Tailwaters often remain open even during the winter in those sections directly below the dam.

velocity of the water being released into the river, and any tributaries that may be contributing colder flows to the tailwater.

Although fishing is technically possible twelve months a year on many of the tailwaters near where I live in Colorado, I've come to find that certain months, most often December and January, are generally just too extreme for me. This doesn't mean that there won't be a day or two where I can get on the water, but it does mean that the average air temperature doesn't get quite high enough during those months. I find that if the air temperature doesn't manage to get up into the upper 30-degree range, little technical problems like frostbite and keeping the ice out of the rod guides can sometimes spoil the fun.

The skills you need for winter fly fishing on the tailwaters actually aren't any different from those that nurtured you through the warmer months. What you will notice is that the river and the life in it moves with a different speed in the winter. If you're lucky you'll also notice that you have the river to yourself, and if for no other reason, this is why you should give "frostbite" fishing a shot.

The first thing you learn about frostbite fishing is that you don't need to set your alarm clock. There's simply no reason to arrive at the

Fly Fishing the Tailwaters

river at the crack of dawn in the winter. Expect the trout to be most active around midday. The pattern I've noted on several western tailwaters on sunny days with air temperatures in the 40s is that nymphing activity begins to pick up around ten or eleven o'clock in the morning and often continues, on and off, into the late afternoon. I look for the midges to begin coming off in the afternoon. The length of winter midge hatches and the degree of the trout's response to them is dependent on many factors. I've seen the midging last an hour one afternoon and on the very next day I've cast to trout that continued rising after dark.

You should expect that nymphing, followed closely by midging, will be your mainstay in the winter months. If you fish the tailwaters enough in the winter, sooner or later you notice that you can generally depend on the trout to rise to a fairly regular afternoon midge hatch. There are those occasions when the midges come off like gangbusters and other times when you can't buy a dimple or a flash or a swirl. It just happens that way sometimes and I don't know anybody who knows why. If you're really lucky there is always the chance, particularly late in the season, of encountering a Blue-Winged Olive hatch or some other small, hardy mayfly coming off the water. Once I fished a rogue hatch of Pale Morning Duns that came off the water in a March snowstorm. You never know.

In regard to nymphing, you can usually expect to find the trout in the deeper holes. Tailwater flow rates tend to be low during the winter and the water remains quite clear. The deeper water is a natural place of refuge for the trout. Having all the trout stacked up in a few deep holes and channels can be a mixed blessing. Although seeing all those trout certainly gets the adrenaline flowing, it also increases the chances of inadvertently snagging one while dead drifting your nymph through the hordes of trout. The trout's metabolisms are lower in the wintertime because of the cold water. This only increases the chances of "false hooking."

Generally, you won't have problems with snagging if you just dead drift the imitation through the run, then lift it gently at the end of the drift. If you add the sharp snap at the end of the drift that many fly fishermen believe attract strikes, there is a very good chance of snagging a fish. Unfortunately there are fly fishermen who get their grins by butt hooking trout when they're stacked up during the winter months. Mistakes happen, but purposeful snagging not only threatens the resource, it's uncool.

This leads into the idea of bringing trout to net as quickly as possible when fly fishing in the winter. It isn't too difficult because the fish tend to be less active in the colder temperatures, anyway. By bringing a trout in quickly and making sure that it is *completely* revived before it is released back into the river, you do not totally deplete its metabolic reserves, which can be stressed more easily in the winter.

For my money, the winter midging that is to be had on many tailwaters is what makes it all worthwhile. For years I ran with a gang of fly fishermen that met every winter and early spring on the South Platte River in Cheeseman Canyon. Although we always made a day of it by spending our morning nymphing the runs and pools in an often less than enthusiastic manner, we lived for the midges that came off the Family Pool like clockwork every afternoon. The hatches tended to be on the heavy side, and at times as much as half the pool was covered in dimpling rises.

The plan was always the same. No matter where we were on the river, we all shambled back to the Family Pool around one in the afternoon when the hatch started. The pool could only reasonably handle three fishermen, so those of us who were left built a warming fire on the shore and waited our turn when one of the other anglers would come out of the river to warm up. These trout weren't ever easy, but on a normal afternoon you could expect to land maybe three or four and hook at least double or triple that many. Not only did we have the whole river to ourselves, but we also were able to solve all the problems of the world when we were standing by the fire. Finicky midging trout, a warming fire, and a small band of fishing pals. What more can you ask for?

Tactics for winter midgers are similar to standard midging principles. If you think the trout wouldn't move much to take a pupa imitation in the spring or summer, wait until you try to move them in the winter. One possible advantage that winter midgers have is that the naturals seem to take more time getting out of their shucks in the colder water and air temperatures, which gives you a few additional casting opportunities to the rising trout. In terms of playing time and the releasing of these trout, the same principles that apply to trout caught nymphing apply here.

Fly Fishing the Tailwaters

Anglers who fish the tailwaters in the winter months need to carry adequate clothing to meet all weather conditions.

An important consideration for all frostbite fly fishermen is the clothes they wear. Let's face it, there are those people who think wading rivers in the middle of winter is not the sanest thing you might do. Fly fishing the tailwaters in winter shouldn't be taken lightly. A fall into the river by an unprepared angler could result in a life-threatening situation that could very well cut into the midging—which is why you're there in the first place. A simple rule is to take more warm clothing than you think you need *and* fire-starting materials.

What you take in the way of extra clothing is an individual decision. I know some anglers who take a complete change of clothing, while others take an extra jacket or sweater and figure if they fall in they'll build a warming fire to dry their clothes. It's up to you. Just remember when making your plans to assume that sooner or later you'll fall or slide into the river. I know that among our little gang on the South Platte there wasn't one of us who escaped standing buck naked around the warming fire while his clothes dried.

Once you have what you think you need in the event of a dunking, you should consider what you need to be as comfortable as possible

Special Cases and Curiosities

while you're fishing. Chest-high neoprene waders are a real plus. Pile pants underneath with a pair of polypropylene long johns next to the skin are excellent, as are the polypropylene long johns with a pair of expedition-weight long johns over them. On top I like to wear a light polypropylene top under a wool long-john top with both covered by a wool shirt. As an outer garment, I use a heavy wool sweater that can be covered by my hooded rainjacket if the weather gets nasty or windy. Another very useful item of clothing is a simple unlined nylon windbreaker. They are lightweight and can really increase the warming capabilities of any combination of clothing when worn as an inner layer.

You should expect your hands to get a little cold now and then no matter what you do. It's just hard to avoid when you're breaking ice out of guides and reviving trout in the water. There are a number of neoprene gloves on the market now that are an improvement over the old fingerless wool gloves. You should pay attention to how your hands feel. When they start getting too cold get out of the water and warm them.

For my head, I wear a simple wool knit watchman's cap that I pull down over my long billed fisherman's cap a la Art Flick. Your feet are a potential source of discomfort, and if they become cold the odds are the rest of you will. Wear polypropylene socks next to the skin, then put on a heavy wool sock or even a couple of socks over them. The most important thing to remember about your feet is to loosen your wading shoes if you wear stocking-foot waders. Tightly laced wading shoes, or wading shoes that are too small, are the most common cause of cold feet among fishermen who use stocking-foot waders.

As far as hazards go, keep your eyes open for the ice that tends to form in the slow water around the edges of pools. I know from experience that if you happen to step on it wrong it makes a wonderful slide right into the pool. You should also watch for the other edge of that ice when you're wading out in the pool—it can be amazingly sharp and can cut you or your waders.

The key safety consideration for fly fishing the tailwaters in the winter is simply moderation. Don't stand out in the river fishing the midges so long that your buddies have to come out and carry you to shore because your legs won't work. If you start to get cold, take a break and warm yourself up. Keep an eye on your pals, too. If they start getting a little weirder than usual, make sure they aren't hypothermic. It's all really just common sense and like Archie Best says, "I like fishing too much to get killed at it. Besides, death takes away from your fishing time."

BOUNCING WATER FLOW RATES

Another twist that you will come across fishing the tailwaters is one that you probably won't find quite as delightful as a winter's afternoon spent midging. It's when the powers that be decide to start messing with the water flow rate. This can come in any number of forms. Most predictable are the somewhat higher but controlled springtime releases from many water-storage reservoirs. These only tend to get out of hand during big water years when you have water coming over the spillway, which in effect gives you an unregulated river.

Anglers who fish hydroelectric tailwaters get used to changes in water flow rates, and although they aren't that easily predicted on any kind of seasonal basis, you can usually find out the power generation schedule for the coming week by contacting the utility people. A general rule of thumb is that power is generated during the day on weekdays but usually isn't generated at night or on the weekends, which often fits nicely into a working angler's schedule. The simple truth about fly fishing many hydroelectric tailwaters when power is being generated is that it may not be worth your time. It's better to call ahead and plan your trip for periods of low water-flow rates.

Facilities that are used only during periods of peak energy consumption or as backups are virtually impossible to predict. When it comes to predicting water-flow rates in this sort of tailwater, you just have to hope that the three-day float trip you scheduled a year in advance doesn't happen to fall on the same day that the old Number Two turbine up the line conks out.

The most difficult tailwater fishing situations don't necessarily occur when flow levels are changed but more often when the flows are "bounced." This is the sort of situation where one day a flow might be 100 cubic feet per second (cfs), then it's raised to 1,000 cfs for three or four days, then dropped again for a few days, and so on. It seems like, at least in the West, managers have become a little more sensitive to this, particularly on the big-money tailwaters that account for hundreds of thousands of angler hours per season. Even taking this into account, the bottom line is that if you fish the tailwaters enough, sooner or later you'll get bounced on. It makes for a difficult fishing situation on the more constant-flow tailwaters where the trout aren't as accustomed to flow rate changes as they would be on a hydroelectic tailwater. The normal response is that they go off the feed for a day or two until they figure out what is going on. When the trout do recover it can sometimes result in a feeding frenzy, most often on nymphs and/or scuds that have been washed into the drift—as long as the flows haven't been changed again in the meantime.

FISHING THE HIGH FLOWS

Longer periods of high flow rates can be expected on many tailwaters in the spring and can provide excellent fly fishing opportunities for the versatile angler. I say *versatile* because there's a syndrome among anglers who regularly fish a particular tailwater where the flows don't change very often. When the water comes up in the spring they stay home because the fishing is "off."

What's happened with many of these fishermen is that they have "wired" the tailwater for its most common flow rate. They've learned an array of riffles, shelves, runs, glides, and pools where they *know* they can catch trout as long as the flow rate is at its regular 1,000 cfs. Many of them just spend their time shuffling back and forth between these spots catching trout. Some of them have caught the same trout so many times in one hole that they name it. If you're fishing with them they'll come up to a run and say, "I wonder what old Oscar's up to today," or, "George was looking a little sick on Monday, didn't fight so hard. Hope he's okay."

Anyway, when the flow rates come up to, say, 4,500 cfs, these guys are lost because the trout have moved and their fish-finding skills are a little rusty. The moral here is that it's better to get skunked trying to find

Fly Fishing the Tailwaters

trout in new places than to spend all your time with a trout named Oscar.

The main thing you want to keep in mind when the water is up is that the trout seek refuge from the heavy water. They also feed heartily on what the increased flow is bringing them.

In many cases the high flow rate throws the hatches completely out of whack and you should then concentrate on nymphing. Work the edges of slower-moving water where the flow spreads into large pools. Don't be afraid to drift a nymph right in next to the bank in six inches of slow water. Try behind rocks where the brunt of the current's velocity is deflected. Add weight to the leader and dead drift in the washes *under* the fast water. Look for any place where it seems a trout could get away from the crushing flow and benefit from trout food caught up in the drift.

I generally stick to standard nymph patterns in high flow-rate situations unless I find evidence that scuds or aquatic worms are in the drift. I do tend to use larger-size imitations, and I definitely beef up my tippet size. High water is also a good time to experiment with dead drifting bigger attractor patterns such as Woolly Buggers, leeches, and Woolly Worms. Try anything that responds with action in the water. Once you find trout in high water, work that section thoroughly, trying different drifts and amounts of weight on the leader and/or fly. The trout will often stack up in optimal lies during high water.

When you're tired of nymphing spend a little time checking out the backwaters and newly flooded areas that occur when flow rates are increased. Although hatches of mayflies and even the hardier caddisflies can be off, these sloughs and backwaters can be the sites of incredible midge activity.

I remember having the San Juan River below Navajo Dam virtually to myself one spring when flow rates were increased to about 5,000 cfs from the normal flow at that time of about 1,200 cfs. It didn't take me long to realize that my wired spots were going to be worthless. I was walking around trying to find fish when I noticed a channel that cut through a flat of cattails. It had been flooded with about eight or nine inches of water. Along the edges of that channel, trout were making the most subtle dimpling rises to midges that I had ever seen. It turned out to be a "hog farm" where I took several 3-pound and 4-pound trout on midge pupa imitations tied on stout little #18 Mustad 3906 hooks.

I took midging trout from that channel and a number of sloughs and backwaters for as long as the water levels stayed up. When things finally got back to normal several weeks later and the flows came down, I wasn't celebrating like a lot of the regulars. Even in the holes I had wired, I never took trout like that!

FISHING LOW WATER SITUATIONS

Low water situations in tailwaters below water-storage reservoirs are most likely to occur in the late summer and can last well into the winter months. From a nympher's point of view the trout will tend to congregate in the deeper channels and holes. If water levels are so low that temperature becomes a factor, look for trout where any springs or tributaries come in, and in deeper shaded channels. Heat stress may cause the trout to go off the feed a bit. Inadvertently snagging trout that have congregated in areas of cooler water is possible. Low, clear water also means that nymphers should approach trout cautiously and take care to wear unobtrusively colored clothing.

Even in low water conditions you can still expect hatches of representative mayfly and caddisfly species on any particular tailwater, although they may be curtailed to some degree in periods of extremely low water. Fishing these hatches doesn't require any special techniques or tactics other than allowing for the fact that the trout are bound to be spookier in the low water. This means gentle, quiet approaches. Good casts and light terminal tackle are also required.

TAILWATER TURNOVER

Another condition that some anglers believe affects tailwater fly fishing is the spring and fall turnover typical in deeper reservoirs. These turnovers occur when water layers in the reservoirs, which thermally stratify during the winter and summer, mix when seasonal changes in air temperatures help to equalize water temperatures and break down the stratification.

The only real complaint I've ever heard about the supposed effect of the turnover is that there is more organic and inorganic debris in the discharge from the reservoir into the river. It is said that this puts the trout off. All the junk in the water can also make dead drift nymphing a chore when you're cleaning off your leader and fly after every cast. I've only experienced one fishing situation on a tailwater where the turnover may have been a factor. This occurred in the springtime and could just as easily have been the effect of increased springtime flows. I've never noted any effects from the fall turnovers. But don't totally dismiss either of them—you never know, and it's a great story to fall back on. It can cover you if you get skunked in the spring or the fall.

SPAWNING RUNS

In the tailwaters where they occur in the spring and/or fall, spawning runs are an important event on many anglers' calendars. On initial examination it may appear that the runs of very large trout out of the reservoirs and into the inflowing streams are not in the realm of tailwater fly fishing because these trout are moving into rivers *above* the dams. Closer study reveals that many tailwaters are actually part of an entire system of dams and tailwaters in a drainage. It seems like once the dam building starts it seldom ends with just one dam. Spawners often migrate upriver from one reservoir until they are stopped by the dam at the next reservoir. The South Platte River in Colorado is a prime example of this with five dams already in place and the specter of the controversial Two Forks Dam still looming as of this writing. The South Platte is also a good example of some awesome spawning runs, particularly out of Elevenmile Reservoir.

Actually, you can usually expect some sort of spawning activity whether the spawners are coming out of a reservoir or are just resident fish moving upstream when the spawning urge hits them. As a general rule the natural expectation is for rainbows and cutthroats to spawn in the spring and browns and brookies to be on the move in the autumn. I say *general* rule because there are notable exceptions, particularly among the various hatchery strains of rainbows whose populations have

Special Cases and Curiosities   139

been manipulated to spawn in the fall. Although these spawning runs are seldom successful in terms of reproduction, they can afford excellent fly fishing opportunities. The Missouri River below Toston Dam is noted for its fall spawning run of rainbow and brown trout that come up out of Canyon Ferry Reservoir into the river.

I view fly fishing to spawning runs a lot like I view fly fishing the high lakes here in Colorado. It's one of those deals where one day you may just knock them out but on the next you can't even buy a strike. I also figure that isn't too high a price to pay for the chance of seeing a 26-inch or 28-inch rainbow trout or a 6-pound to 8-pound brown, let alone getting a shot at landing one.

I have an advantage on many of the spawning runs I fish because the tailwaters these trout are running into are clear enough and shallow enough that I can sight-fish to the spawners. This removes the problem of finding concentrations of spawners that are often encountered on bigger water where the fish can't be seen as easily. Unfortunately, visually finding the trout *doesn't* remove the problem of whether or not they're in a striking mood.

There are a lot of theories about what these brutish spawners want. Some anglers go by the theory that the trout are very territorial during spawning and if you can throw something in front of them like a Woolly Bugger or a Zonker, they will strike it just out of spite or to move it from their path. Other anglers stick to egg patterns borrowed from steelhead fishermen. The egg patterns might be the best overall pattern to use on spawners, although many fly fishermen don't consider them quite as sporting as other patterns. Other anglers just fish the same patterns to the spawners that they always use on the river. You ask what's the best? Well, I've caught spawners on every one of the patterns I have just listed. I've probably done the best with Woolly Buggers, but I've caught my share on egg patterns, too. I've even landed a few early season spawners on midge pupa imitations.

I guess my gut feeling is that if you find the spawners in the mood you will probably be able to find something in your fly box that they'll take. More importantly, it pays to be on the water when it's most likely the spawners are hitting. This means early in the morning and late in the afternoon on sunny days and throughout the day on cloudy or rainy

Fly Fishing the Tailwaters

days. My best luck with spawners has always occurred on days when the weather was pretty miserable.

MYSIS SHRIMP MYSTERIES

Among tailwater curiosities, the one that stands out in my mind the most is the bizarre story of Mysis shrimp. Although these shrimp aren't particularly widespread in tailwaters throughout the country, their story is interesting if just to show that even the best laid plans can go astray, or at least turn out a lot different than you ever thought they would. When I asked a fisheries biologist here in Colorado to explain the Mysis shrimp story to me he started off by saying, "Oh, that dark and stormy night...."

The story goes that *Mysis relicta* occur naturally in northern-latitude lakes, like Great Slave and Yellowknife, across the Canadian Shield and over into Scandinavia and Russia. The shrimp are the sole freshwater representatives of a shrimp that is usually found in salt water and is believed to have been stranded inland after the last Ice Age. Anyway, their home waters tend to be those very deep, sterile, cold northern lakes, where they eat anything they can get but have a marked preference for tiny freshwater animals called zooplankton.

Biologists noted that the lake trout where these shrimp occurred grew to enormous sizes, along with the kokanee salmon. By the 1950s they were stocking the Mysis shrimp in reservoirs in Colorado and other western states in hopes of providing food for stocked populations of kokanees and lake trout.

It didn't work out exactly that way. The biologists found that, much to their dismay, the kokanee salmon were hardly able to feed on the Mysis shrimp at all. The wily and supremely evolved shrimp migrated up to the surface of the reservoirs at night to feed, and when the sun came out they migrated down to the depths. The shrimp went as deep as they could go, which meant the bottom or until they hit the unoxygenated bottom layers of water.

Since kokanee salmon are almost exclusively sight feeders they weren't able to see the shrimp even in the unlikely event that they cruised the deep, dark waters of the reservoirs. The shrimp are as clear as glass. At nighttime, when the shrimp were near the surface feeding on zooplankton, it was too dark for the kokanees to see them.

This was bad enough in itself, but what was worse was that the Mysis shrimp were particularly fond of a zooplankton called *Daphnia,* which happens to be the major food source of both kokanee salmon and the smaller trouts. So not only was it impossible for the kokanees or trout to eat the Mysis shrimp, but the shrimp also ate up all their food. In terms of trout and kokanee salmon, many of the reservoirs that were stocked with the shrimp could support only put-and-take fisheries or at best very meager populations of fish. The only trout in the reservoir to come out on the plus side were the big lake trout because they are deep-water feeders by nature. The lake trout grew to tremendous sizes where the shrimp were stocked.

The other beneficiaries were the trout who lived in the tailwaters below the reservoirs. The equation was simple. The Mysis shrimp that migrated to the deep water were getting sucked through the bottom-release gates near the dam and dumped into the river below during the daytime when the trout could see them. The growth rates were phenomenal to the point of crudeness.

In the Frying Pan River below Ruedi Reservoir, where Mysis shrimp were stocked heavily, the trout grew into 5-pound, 7-pound, and even 10-pound Mysis-gorged footballs within the first mile or so below the dam. Fly fishermen came up with a number of Mysis shrimp patterns that ranged anywhere from white marabou and Flashabou to clear plastic bags tied over hooks that had been wrapped in white thread. The fishermen went nuts. They were pulling trout out of the Frying Pan—which was a fine little trout stream in its own right before the dam and before the Mysis shrimp—that were as big in terms of pounds as those steelhead fishermen caught. I say in terms of pounds, because Mysis-fed trout are characteristically rather short in length but of tremendous girth. That's why they call them footballs.

The glut of monster trout certainly brought a surge of anglers to the Frying Pan, along with an infusion of an estimated one million bucks into the local economy. More recently though, there has been a certain measure of pining for the old predam Frying Pan River that Ernest Schwiebert described so affectionately in *Matching the Hatch,* and even the pre-Mysis shrimp Frying Pan when it was simply a tailwater below the Ruedi Dam. It's also interesting to note that the pining occurs almost exclusively among those anglers who have landed a couple of the footballs. Anyway, the hog trout are up there near the dam for those who choose to go after them. Downstream, the Frying Pan turns into just another wonderful tailwater fishery.

How did this all happen? The kokanees *did* feed on Mysis shrimp up in Canada, didn't they? Here is the scuttlebutt. The story goes that the large Mysis-fed kokanees occurred in one bay of one lake up in Canada where a rogue current caused an upwelling that brought the shrimp to the surface of the shallow bay in the daylight where the kokanees could get them! The biologists just didn't know that at the time. But they do now. It really was just a bit of bad luck. Of all the lakes in which to look at kokanee populations, the one aberrant example happened to be chosen. All the biologists ever really wanted to do was grow bigger kokanees.

It could have been worse. The lake-trout fishermen certainly aren't disappointed. And if you haven't landed a Mysis-fed tailwater trout or two, it's better not to say anything until you do. They really are something....

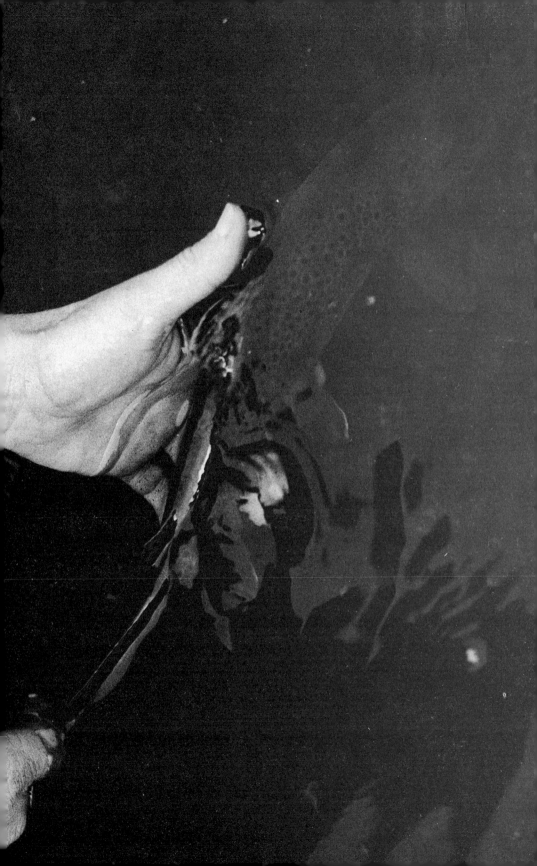

CHAPTER 8

The Enigma–Loving Tailwaters to Death

T HE SAN JUAN RIVER just below Navajo Dam is a unique tailwater in a number of ways. There is a section characterized not by the typical single channel with a gravel bar here and there, but rather by a main channel that sidles up to a myriad of braided mini-channels, slots, holes, backwater sloughs, and flats.

While most of the anglers content themselves with working the channels and holes where dead drifting San Juan worms and scud, nymph, and midge pupa imitations is highly effective, there is a special kind of fishing to be had out on the cattail-encircled flats. Big rainbows lie in the mere wisps of current that slide into the flats off the channels. Some of the big fish spend their time casually picking off midge pupa, while others cruise erratically over the flats taking emerging nymphs and even an occasional snail. Meticulous anglers who make careful approaches and well-planned casts and hold their ground against trout running into the weed beds can occasionally land hard-earned heavy trout.

There's more to the flats than just big fish, too. For those of us who can't quite afford the bonefish and permit at Key West or who just haven't made it to the salt water with a fly rod yet, these flats are a place for fantasy. When the early June sun makes everything bright and hot down on the water, we think maybe it is something like this out on the saltwater flats. Sometimes, for just a minute or two, the thought crosses our minds that maybe we have it all.

That's the way I was feeling one afternoon on the "Juan." I'd taken a trout or two by lightly casting a little Gold-Ribbed Hare's Ear here and there to the cruisers and then, after it had drifted four or five inches

Heavy fishing pressure on many blue-ribbon tailwater fisheries has necessitated the introduction of special regulations to preserve them.

under the surface, slowly hand-twisting it back. It was the kind of slow, patient work that can sometimes pay off for a fly fisherman. After I'd released the second fish, I noticed out of the corner of my eye some fishermen who were working the braids, watching me.

Maybe it wasn't even from the corner of my eye, because I think I might have been overcome with that cocky sort of exhilaration that comes when you hook up with a trout. It was the kind of fish that while you're playing it, you glance quickly from side to side, hoping that there might be a "gallery." I probably considered tipping my hat to the other anglers, but that's really only the sort of thing I do under the influence of a heavy adrenaline rush and probably not even then. But you know how it is when it comes to a good fish.

After I took a third fish, the other anglers, together and almost on cue, came out of the channels and began drifting toward my flat with a determined kind of walk that said, "You got all the trout over there, huh?" Before long they were edging closer and closer to me. None of them had rerigged after coming in from nymphing the channels. They were plunking heavily weighted nymphs, set up for dead drifting, in the

Fly Fishing the Tailwaters

almost currentless flat. It put the trout down immediately, and they couldn't help but goo up their nymphs with algae on every cast. I'd been tailwater "mugged" as sure as shooting, so I went on my way.

I don't know what those fishermen were thinking when they came over but I doubt they had any malicious intentions. They probably just wanted to get in on the fishing. Maybe no one had ever mentioned to them that it's not sporting to crowd a dreamy fly fisherman off the flats. Even though the San Juan has developed a bit of a reputation as a muggers' river, especially during the busy times on the weekends, you can't blame everything on a few ill-mannered fishermen. A tailwater can only support so many anglers at a given time before somebody's dreams are shattered.

I started this book off talking about the San Juan River and it seems only fitting to wind things up there, too. The simple truth is that the San Juan really does represent the best of what many tailwaters have to offer in terms of trout fishing. It is a hyperproductive aquatic environment that not only sustains huge numbers of trout but also produces good numbers of very large trout, and fishes well year-round. It also represents many of the problems that are beginning to surface at the most popular tailwater fisheries, particularly in the western states.

CROWDED TAILWATERS

What we're talking about here are tailwaters that may sustain one hundred thousand angler days or more a year. These are the rivers that are so productive and so enticing that they attract fly fishermen from across the country. They are also the rivers that produce shoulder-to-shoulder fishing and "hatches" of float fishermen during peak times. They are the rivers that make you wonder if there's a limit to the pressure a tailwater can take in relation to the resource itself and in regard to the quality of experience.

It all started to dawn on me one summer when I found myself getting up at four in the morning so that I could be on the San Juan at sunup, catch the midge hatch, and be off the river before the crowds showed up around eight or nine. I noticed it on the South Platte River in Colorado when I was spending more time fishing in winter and early spring than

during the summer. It cropped up again when I began to chart in my fishing log not only the hatches, but also the number of anglers on the river so that I could get a fix on the "empty" days. In my case it turned out Tuesday was the best weekday. Also, those hardy weekend anglers who didn't give a damn about how they'd feel at work on Monday morning and stayed on for the Sunday evening fishing could just about plan on having the river to themselves.

If you look at the growth of interest in fly fishing during the last decade or so it's hard to expect anything else. Various sources indicate that the *business* of fly fishing is growing at a rate of 10 to 15 percent a year. That may not translate directly into numbers of new fly fishermen, but it's a good indication that either more fly fishermen are heading to

Fly Fishing the Tailwaters

Crowded conditions on the more popular tailwaters require that anglers respect each other's rights.

the rivers and lakes every season or that those of us who already fly fish are spending a hell of a lot more money.

The greater numbers of fly fishermen haven't been all bad for the tailwaters, either. In a number of cases, fly fishermen along with fisheries biologists have successfully advocated regulations to preserve tailwater trout populations. The result is that you find very few major tailwater trout fisheries in the United States that don't at least have slot limits. Many tailwaters have strict catch-and-release and barbless-hooks-only regulations. Others limit anglers to a couple of trout of a certain size a day or maybe to one trophy trout of, say, 20 inches or more.

More important than the regulations themselves is the fact that many fly fishermen, through the influence of a number of national conservation groups, voluntarily limit the number of trout that they kill, if they choose to kill any at all.

The special regulations on many tailwaters have a curious result that reminds me of the effect that a wilderness designation in the national forests tended to have in the 1970s and early 1980s. If you wanted to quadruple the usage of any unspoiled area, all you had to do was designate it a wilderness. In terms of fly fishermen and tailwaters it seems as if a catch-and-release designation has about the same effect. Fly fishermen *know* that in all probability a tailwater requiring all fish to be returned unharmed to the river will be home to more trout, and most importantly, larger trout. It draws the crowds for certain. A more ominous difference that the special regulations make on the tailwaters is that unlike a wilderness where people can spread out a little to lessen the impact, a tailwater is only so many miles long. The special regulations tend to concentrate fly fishermen rather than disperse them.

It is important to note that crowding is a relative term. I've made a few tailwater fishing trips on the weekends with friends from the eastern states where I was ready to pull out my hair because of the crowds while they were marveling at how much "open" water was available to fish. I guess some of us in the West get a little snooty if we even *see* another angler anywhere on the river! You can be sure we're learning, though. More importantly, I think we need to understand that limits do exist.

GOOD TAILWATER MANNERS

As the tailwaters become more crowded, anglers need to become more sensitive to their fellow fishermen. What we're talking about here is simple manners. Although equally correct, I like to stay away from using the term "stream etiquette" in matters of this nature. Whenever I hear the term, I expect to see Amy Vanderbilt coming around the bend in hippers carrying a cane rod.

I like thinking of streamside manners more in terms of those first days afield with a shotgun that I spent with my father. There were just some things that you were *required* to know if you wanted to be among other hunters. Dad passed down ideas about conduct that were necessary for the safety of other bird hunters. These were simple courtesies you would want another hunter to extend to you, such as not pointing a gun at your head or swinging up on a bird too close to you. In times past, the tenets of streamside courtesy were, in fact, passed from father to son. More recently, the better fly fishing instructors have taken on the burden.

Streamside manners, like hunting courtesies, are just common-sense considerations. Of course, neglecting to observe streamside courtesies usually results in less deadly consequences, unless your disregard of protocol is responsible for putting down a trout that another angler has been meticulously working over for the past three hours. The most basic tenet of streamside courtesy is simple enough. You don't disturb the water that another angler is actively working or resting. The resting of a certain stretch of water is the more difficult of the two to figure out because in many crowded tailwater fishing situations you often come across anglers sitting idly by the stream. In these cases it doesn't hurt to ask if the water is being rested. The more subtle nuances of not disturbing another fly fisherman's water come into play when you pass an angler actively working a stretch of water. Keep your shadow off the

Fly Fishing the Tailwaters

water in areas where it might spook the trout and, if possible, get out of the water altogether to pass. If you must wade, wade as carefully as you would if you were approaching a rising trout.

A fine line differentiates how close is too close to another angler. Obviously, fishing through the water of another party is bound to cause problems, but you may also be on thin ice if you begin casting your dry fly closer and closer to the drift that another fly fisherman is working.

If you find yourself fishing a stretch of water that does support two or more anglers comfortably and a fellow angler hooks a fish, you should reel in your line to prevent tangles while the trout is being played. Move from your spot if you find yourself in the way of the fisherman playing the trout. There is no better way to make friends streamside than to reel in when another angler is playing a trout close by. It also puts you in position to wade over and admire the fish if it is successfully brought to net.

I know what you're thinking if you've experienced a crowded day on any of the big-time tailwaters. You're thinking that all these "traditional" time-honored courtesies were fine and dandy back in the 1930s and 1940s when fly fishermen were kinder and gentler, but today's tailwater fishing is different. It's a dog-eat-dog world out there. If you're not on your toes you may never get to cast over the better water. You figure that if you move out of the way of an angler who's playing the best trout he has ever hooked in his life, some jerk who doesn't give a damn about that fisherman's ecstasy will move into *your* spot.

Okay, the world has changed. There are a lot of reasons. In some cases it's as simple as the word not getting passed along. Some fishermen just don't know how to act. It's not that they're trying to be jerks. That's easy enough to fix. Other problems may be a little harder to overcome. There is no place in the country where it's more apparent that fly fishing techniques have changed than on the tailwaters.

A big change has been the almost universal adoption of dead drift nymphing techniques. Although you will still encounter the occasional argument over whether dead drift nymphing is fly fishing at all, most anglers now agree that the technique broadens and enhances their sport. On some tailwaters where hatches are less prolific, dead drift nymphing is the technique of choice for many anglers.

A problem with dead drift nymphing in many areas is that it jams anglers up on the channels, slots, and holes. Fishermen will literally "park" on one productive run for an entire day. I once saw a group of fly fishermen working a particularly hot run on a cold spring afternoon. Two anglers would nymph until they were too cold to continue at which time their two fishing buddies on the shore would change places with them. By switching back and forth they prevented access by any other anglers to that spot for the entire day. If you listened hard enough you could hear the grumbling up and down the river. Once or twice I've seen situations like this almost come to violence.

Parking to this degree is relatively new to fly fishing. While certain favorable spots were occasionally hogged in the past, the rule in fly fishing tended toward movement on an angler's part. Fly fishermen worked their way upstream or downstream, covering water by casting dry flies, wet flies, or weighted nymphs. Anglers worked a variety of water types in a day ranging from runs to riffles to pools. If they encountered favorable responses they lingered, and when the action died down they continued on.

On today's tailwaters, basic dead drift nymphing techniques make fly fishing a more stationary endeavor, as does the nature of the tailwater itself, where trout often congregate heavily in the runs, channels, and deeper pools. Although this has always been the case, even in unregulated rivers, the high productivity of many tailwaters may place enough trout in a single good run that an experienced nympher can spend his entire day catching trout in that one spot. This means that trout and nymphers are often literally stacked up in the runs like cordwood. This condition is only exacerbated in low water conditions.

Conditions similar to those encountered with dead drift nymphing are beginning to occur during midge hatches, which can sometimes last the better part of a day. Once the province of only the most skilled and probably the most fanatic anglers, increasing numbers of fly fishermen are now finding their way into the subtle delicacies of midging. Again, fly fishermen often park on particularly productive waters to the day-long exclusion of all other anglers.

The courtesies necessary for these kinds of fly fishing situations haven't really developed yet, where might seems to be right, and possession is 90 percent of the law. Life could be a lot simpler on many crowded tailwaters if nymphers, and in some cases midgers, just followed the same common-sense rules of previous years. If other anglers are waiting for a chance, why not take a few good trout from a run then give them a shot? There's plenty of river out there, and on the tailwaters you never know where you might find trout.

Real satisfaction often comes from the ability to fish a variety of water types rather than just knowing where you can yank a trout out of a run on a deep drifted nymph. There's usually plenty of pocket water, shallow riffles, and backwaters where you can put your trout-searching techniques to use. If big trout are your trip, you will often be amazed at the weird places you will find them, too. The key to all of this is that you don't have to measure the success of your day by the number of trout you catch.

SNAGGING, SHUFFLING, AND POACHING

Aside from streamside manners, a few general ethical questions regarding the tailwaters arise. Dead drift nymphing gets the rap here once again. This time it has to do with that small group of people who snag trout on purpose. Once you learn the ins and outs of nymphing it won't be long before you realize that in certain cases you can snag fish if you want. I'm not talking about the times when you inadvertently snag a fish on the outside of the jaw, the cheek, or the pectoral fin because you were late setting up on the trout. In most cases where a trout is foul hooked in those areas the odds are that the fish actually took the imitation and probably rejected it while you were detecting and reacting to the strike. It happens to everybody. Sometimes you might even foul hook a trout in the dorsal fin or tail by mistake.

I'm talking about the cases where some clown is sight-nymphing a run that is crammed with trout and every fish he lands is hooked in the butt. The dead giveaway to intentional snagging is when the guy closely follows the lead weight on his leader as it drifts downstream. When it's in the pack of fish he strikes hard, pulling the hook sharply through the water. Odds are, particularly in low water situations, that he'll connect and a trout will scream out of the channel stripping out fly line and maybe even backing. Even a 10-inch trout hooked in the butt puts up quite a battle.

More conscientious nymphers will make it a point to strike briskly but very short. It doesn't take much to set a hook when you're nymphing. Other nymphers follow Lefty Kreh's advice and strike *down* when nymphing. This sets the hook twice as fast. If you don't believe me, or actually Lefty, put together a rod and strike up in the normal fashion while watching the rod tip. You'll notice that it goes down first, adding a little slack to your rig for the microsecond or so before the rod tip goes up. If you try again, striking down this time, you'll see the rod tip go up first, which would set the hook in a nymphing situation.

You may think that I sure know a lot about butt hooking trout for a guy who is preaching ethics. You're right, folks. The fact is that in my younger years I sometimes would get so frustrated when I couldn't get one out of the fifty feeding trout in a run to strike my nymph imitation that I would try to snag them. It wasn't hard. I might have even thought it was a little cool when other anglers would chime out, "What're you using?" I gave up on it when I started seeing more and more trout that were beaten, scarred, and covered with the fungus resulting from being foul hooked.

Now if I foul hook a fish, which can happen early in the season before my reflexes have sharpened, it embarrasses me to the point where I sometimes apologize to the other fishermen. The moral of this story is that if you can't catch the trout, try to figure out what they're eating and then go home and tie some flies—don't take out your frustrations on the fish by butt hooking and damaging them.

A more recent development in the areas of tailwater "sin" has taken its name from the San Juan River, although you see it in tailwaters across the country. It's called the San Juan shuffle and it's now illegal in all designated Special Trout Waters in New Mexico. The shuffle got its name when some fly fishermen on the San Juan were seen constantly shuffling around and kicking up debris from the streambed.

As it turns out they didn't have a case of itchy athlete's foot. Actually, they were kicking up the very rich nymphal forms of aquatic insect life that live in the substrate on the San Juan. Shuffling all those bugs into the drift was better than chumming in terms of attracting and concentrating trout. Sometimes there were so many fish that they bumped into these guys' legs.

Fly Fishing the Tailwaters

Regulations that permit the legal taking of one trophy trout, like this 23-inch San Juan River rainbow, are often violated when fishermen kill smaller, non-legal trout that they haven't measured but believe meet trophy standards.

I still remember the first time I ran into shuffling anglers on the San Juan, because I couldn't figure out what they were doing. I saw these guys dancing around with a circle of cloudy water around them and fishing *downstream*. They were pulling in trout right and left. I tend to be a little naive about things like this and started going through my fly boxes looking for wet flies. I thought there had been a revival of the gentle art of wet fly fishing right there on my home river! It was quite a while before I figured out what was really going on.

Nowadays, there's a game warden down on the San Juan who drives around in an unmarked truck with a spotting scope attached to an old rifle stock. He spends his time looking for shufflers and busting them if he can. They should have stuck to wet flies.

Poaching is an ever-present threat on many tailwaters simply because the special regulations that are in effect, along with the richness of the waters, provide for the growth of trophy trout. Poaching may not occur in the classic nightstalker fashion but rather in situations where regulations allow the keeping of one trophy trout. Often, well-intentioned anglers who "forgot" their tape measure find that the trophy trout they have taken is below the size limit and it ends up in the bushes. The list goes on to snagging fish illegally, use of bait where it's restricted, and all the things those of us who fly fish the busier tailwaters occasionally witness.

Above and beyond manners, ethics, gossip, and vicious rumors, there is some concern about the condition of the trout themselves in heavily pressured tailwaters. Although the fish are returned to the water more or less alive, in many cases the fishing pressure is so intense that wounded, scarred, and sick trout have become considerably more common. Injuries range from split jaws to missing fins, sliced tails, and puncture wounds that occur anywhere on the fish. Many of these injuries come from false hooking incidents while nymphing. A whole other array of injuries occur when trout are improperly handled and then released.

Although the case for barbless hooks has been disputed in terms of making a difference in survival rates for fairly hooked trout, there's no question that fish snagged accidentally in the body suffer less damage when a barbless hook is removed from their flesh than a barbed hook. For my money, barbless hooks are easier on both trout and trout fishermen, and I would make them mandatory on all heavily fished catch-and-release tailwater fisheries.

MINIMUM FLOW IS THE KEY

As much as it may seem, especially on a crowded Saturday morning, that too many fishermen pose the greatest threat to fly fishing in the tailwaters, the reality is that the crowded conditions probably pose more of a threat to the *quality* of the fly fishing. The major threats to the fisheries are posed by poor regulation of water flow rates, which can result in less than adequate water levels in the tailwater. Let's face it, most reservoir managers don't regulate water releases with the trout's welfare as a major priority. Things such as power generation, irrigation water, and nice green lawns in semiarid urban areas like Denver come first. That's the way it has always been.

The most important issue for tailwater trout often boils down to the question of minimum flow. Minimum flow is the lowest rate in cubic feet per second that a tailwater is allowed to flow. In the past these minimum flows were determined based on a number of factors that may or may not have included the needs of the trout. Most often, a primary concern in the setting of minimum flows had to do with downstream obligations to water users. In a tailwater that was running too low in the winter, it was a cinch that water managers didn't consider what the anchor ice would do to next season's mayfly hatches. Most minimum flow standards in the western states, *if* any exist at all, are now set so that a tailwater fishery is not totally destroyed if they are imposed, but they can certainly devastate it to the point that years of recovery may be necessary.

Inadequate flow rates damage the fisheries in a number of ways. In tailwaters where natural reproduction occurs, spawning beds can be left high and dry if water levels drop below a critical point due to inadequate flow rates. The same is true for insect populations. The trout can end up crowded into the deeper holes where they are vulnerable to heavy legal and illegal fishing pressure. Low flows in the summer months can also raise water temperatures to unacceptable levels.

The whole minimum flow question is bound into an intricate web of water law, federal and state bureaucracies, user group requirements, environmental bickering and plain good-old-boy politics. Plain and simple, it's just one big ball of wax. The classic arguments that have so often held up progressive environmental stewardship are seen in force here.

My favorite is: "We'd do something but we just can't get a handle on how to measure recreational use. If you trout fishermen were cows or wheat or timber we could get a handle on what you're worth."

How about one to two million regular fly fishermen and as many as ten million who fish at least once a year? How about the million bucks that gets pumped into a little community along the Frying Pan River?

It's not all doom and gloom. As much as I like having the Bureau of Reclamation as the enemy of tailwater fly fishers, I have to admit that after more than a decade of bickering and occasional open warfare with them, I think their attitude is changing. The *rules* have not changed yet, but attitude is the first step. Bureau of Reclamation administrators seem more open now than ever. Impoundment designs have changed continuously over the years, often to the benefit of tailwater fly fishermen (multi-level gates are a good example). At least the relationship seems a little less adversarial. I've noticed that they have even hired a public affairs officer at one of the local offices I occasionally harass.

Both conservation and environmental groups have become more active in minimum flow questions. Along with monitoring flows, input by these groups early on in the process of determining acceptable minimum flows is important. I'll be the first to admit that I'm not an expert in these questions. I try to make my voice heard when necessary and give a few bucks to groups that I think have an impact. I tend to view the environmental professionals about the same way I view paramedics and ambulance drivers. I don't have the stomach for a lot of it, but I'm glad somebody does. I'll give at the office.

POSSIBLE SOLUTIONS

A relatively new line of thinking among conservationists, which sounds promising, is actually buying water to augment flow rates that get too low and threaten a tailwater system. This search for new alternatives and the stronger involvement of the conservation lobby has come at the right time. Water resources, particularly in drier western states, are being stretched more and more each year.

Regarding the somewhat more benign question of crowding, there are a number of solutions. I noted one several years ago in Wyoming where I saw a fly fisherman with a .357 magnum in a shoulder holster strapped over his fishing vest. The purported idea behind it was for "griz" protection, which it might well have afforded for the once in a lifetime grizzly bear you see in Wyoming, but just wearing it sure kept the casting lanes open.

On specific tailwaters that really get hammered by anglers there are several innovations I could live with. I'd like to see seasonal riverkeepers hired for the busiest months of the year. A riverkeeper could help deter poaching, collect important biological data, and provide educational background to anglers that are new to the tailwater.

Another possibility for relieving angling pressure would be to limit the number of anglers on certain heavily fished sections of river. I'd be willing to take my turn to fish a favorite tailwater if it meant less pressure. It might also pay to close the season during the winter months on

Fly Fishing the Tailwaters

some of the more heavily fished tailwaters. If a period of recovery over the winter months would improve a fishery I'd go along with it.

Despite the fact that there are more of us fly fishing the tailwaters each season, they seem to hold up remarkably well. Some are as rich a fishery as you'll find anywhere in the country, tailwater or not. Some provide fishing for trout where historically there were no trout. Many are home to the persnickety, finicky risers that we all love to curse but secretly can't get enough of. A few tailwaters are tough enough that catching trout there qualifies you to catch trout on almost any river, anywhere.

Sure the tailwaters are productive. You can prove it by attaching a counter to your fishing vest and keeping track of the trout you catch and then release. You can also prove it by leaving the counter at home and spending a dreamy day on the flats. You can prove it by a particular trout that through its craftiness, ingeniousness, or just plain craziness earns your respect. The kind of trout that you end up talking to...a trout that comes to represent the enigma of the very tailwater itself.